TEACHERS MANUAL

TO ACCOMPANY

CASES AND MATERIALS ON ALTERNATIVE DISPUTE RESOLUTION

by

LEO KANOWITZ
Professor of Law
University of California
Hastings College of the Law

St. Paul, Minn.
WEST PUBLISHING CO.
1986

West Publishing Co.
50 West Kellogg Boulevard
P.O. Box 64526
St. Paul, Minnesota 55164-0526

ISBN 0-314-98314-7

TABLE OF CONTENTS

Page

Page

Page

Page

CHAPTER ONE
INTRODUCTION

A. ALTERNATIVE DISPUTE RESOLUTION: BACKGROUND AND OBJECTIVES (Page 1)

Professors who have no objection to using audio-visual materials in class might consider showing the excellent television program on the Alternative Dispute Resolution (ADR) movement, produced by Public Television Station KQED in San Francisco as part of its "Express" series. The program is called "Justice Without Law." As a sort of introduction to the Introduction, it can be especially useful in the first class session. The program, which focuses on San Francisco's Community Boards project, depicts volunteer mediators trained in simulated sessions and a real Community Board in action, mediating in a landlord-tenant dispute. It also includes a simulated divorce mediation session. The documentary portion of this program, which lasts one-half hour, is followed by a half-hour free-wheeling discussion of the attractions and dangers of the ADR movement. The discussants include Attorney Melvin Belli, University of California Anthropology Professor Laura Nader, Nolo Press Publisher Jake Warner and Raymond Shonholtz, the president of the San Francisco Community Boards Project.

"Justice Without Law" comes in a 30 minute version which includes only the documentary portion of the program, and a 60 minute version which includes the documentary and studio discussion. I am informed that the costs for the 30 minute version are: $186.38 for a 3/4" copy and $175.73 for a 1/2" VHS copy. The costs for the 60 minute version are: $213.00 for a 3/4" copy and $202.35 for a 1/2" VHS copy. Checks should be made payable to KQED, Inc, and sent to the attention of Sharon Ellison, Facilities Coordinator, Golden Gate Productions, 500 Eighth Street, San Francisco, CA 94103.

* * *

(Page 1): Does the assertion that "in the absence of an established legal order * * * many, if not most, disputes would either remain unresolved, or would be resolved through the use of force" withstand analysis? Have not people always resorted to dispute resolution mechanisms outside of established judicial systems? Negotiation, for example, has been available and used since time immemorial. Third party neutrals, who are not officials of an established legal order, to help parties arrive at their own negotiated resolution of disputes have also been frequently resorted to in the past. At times, such third parties have served as conciliators or mediators. At other times, the disputing parties have delegated to such non-governmental third parties the authority to hear and finally decide their disputes. Formerly, and even in modern times, the role of third party neutrals has often been performed by religious leaders, neighbors or persons whose occupations or other pursuits have made them knowledgeable about the subject matter of the parties' dispute.

Nevertheless, feelings of anger, frustration or bitterness often prevent disputing parties from seeking a negotiated resolution of their conflict. Similar factors may disable them from enlisting the aid of non-governmental neutral third parties to help them resolve their differences. Under such circumstances, which are probably the rule rather than the exception, the unavailability of an established judicial mechanism for dispute resolution would leave the parties with a stark choice: either to abandon their positions or to resort to self help. Frequently, if not inevitably, the latter option would involve some level of violence.

B. PATHS TO JUSTICE (Page 3)

This report avoids two possible extreme positions regarding the promise and potential of alternative dispute resolution mechanisms. One is espoused by some people who appear to have an unbridled faith in what ADR techniques can achieve. In their view, resort to litigation is to be avoided if humanly possible. Although they do not speak in such terms, they appear to share Jean Jacques Rousseau's perception of the fundamanetal nature of human beings. Under that view, people are born "good;" it is only as a result of living among other people in society that they are corrupted and develop "bad" or "evil" traits. It follows, therefore, that by avoiding the "war-like" atmosphere of litigation, people can resolve their disputes on the basis of reason and good will.

At the other end are those whose view of humanity is reminiscent of that proffered by Thomas Hobbes, the author of "Leviathan." According to Hobbes, people are born evil; only social restraints hold them in check. It is, therefore, logical to place primary reliance for resolving disputes on state-sanctioned litigation processes, or at least the actual or potential threat of invoking them. Whether one talks about international conflict or disputes between individuals or between between individuals and government, their resolution depends upon the availability of law-imposed sanctions for "wrong" behavior. Although reason and good will can influence the outcome of such disputes, it is naive to suggest that such factors can make a crucial difference.

The "Paths to Justice" report steers a middle course between these positions. On the one hand, it recognizes that present-day litigation processes are deficient in important respects--and that mediation and arbitration, among other ADR devices, can provide more satisfying results in many instances. At the same time, it emphasizes that ADR techniques do not represent a cure-all for the ills that beset the current court system; and that, depending upon the discrete circumstances and a weighing of the factors set forth in the report, judicial dispute resolution can often be more beneficial to the individual and to society than an alternative dispute resolution method.

NOTES AND PROBLEMS FOR DISCUSSION (Page 30)

Note 1 (Page 30): It is far from clear that lawyers would be replaced in significant numbers, or at all, if alternative dispute resolution processes were widely adopted in fields that have heretofore been handled exclusively by attorneys. In divorce mediation, for example, to the extent that property and support rights are disputed, lawyers may be indispensable to the process. (See, e.g., Werle v. Rhode Island Bar Association, at p. 105 of the Casebook.) The Mini-Trial, examined in Chapter Six of the Casebook, is another area where the role of lawyers continues to be significant--both in the presentation of the respective parties' cases to the neutral observer and in the discovery process preceding the mini-trial itself. The role of lawyers in labor arbitration is well known; indeed, many have lamented the increasing formalization and legalization of the labor arbitration process. Moreover, many attorneys or would-be attorneys who are attracted to various aspects of ADR processes, will develop specialties as lawyer-mediators or lawyer-arbitrators.

Even if more frequent use of alternative dispute resolution mechanisms were to reduce available work opportunities for lawyers, the nature of the lawyer's primary social responsibility should be explored. Is it to assure the existence of adequate markets for the lawyer's services? Or to assure that people's needs for efficient, inexpensive and equitable dispute resolution mechanisms are satisfied? Are these goals mutually exclusive?

Note 2 (Page 31): With regard to Professor Fiss' observations about settlement, it should be noted first that the "Paths to Justice" report is not insensitive to some of the concerns expressed in them. The report itself recognizes that in many situations judicial dispute resolution is superior to either mediation or arbitration, which are the principal alternative devices it examines. At the same time, there is a significant difference in the dispute resolution mechanisms emphasized by the "Paths to Justice" report and by Professor Fiss. The former appears to prefer non-judicial mechanisms. By contrast, Professor Fiss clearly prefers judicial dispute resolution, allowing for non-judicial alternatives only in exceptional and limited circumstances.

Some of the questions that are relevant to a resolution of these differences are: 1) What proportion of disputed matters that go to trial involve issues requiring judicial explication? 2) Are not many matters that divide parties simply disputed questions of fact, the determination of which is often entrusted by the judicial system to lay jurors? 3) As for enforcement, isn't the settlement agreement itself a contract, which, if a party defaults, can ultimately be relied upon by the other party in a judicial trial? (See, e.g., Press Machinery Corp. v. Smith RPM Corp, reported at page 188 of the Casebook). 4) What measures can be taken to ensure the competence of third-party neutrals? 5) Are trial court judges or juries necessarily more competent than arbitrators or other third-party neutrals to make factual determinations? 6) Does the availability of an appeal adequately protect parties from incorrect findings of fact or law at the trial court level? 7) If a party to a settlement agreement, whether negotiated directly with the opposing party or with the aid of a third-party neutral, wishes to rescind or reform that agreement, under what circumstances can, or should, a court grant such relief? 8) Do the delay and expense of judicial dispute resolution diminish the stature of the courts in the minds of the public? 9) If so, would not their stature be raised if only exceptional, rather than ordinary, disputes were sought to be resolved by them?

The questions raised in the last paragraph of Note 2 are probably best answered after the students have delved more thoroughly into the details of the various dispute resolution devices treated in the book. At this stage, however, one can note some distinctions among these devices that bear on Professor Fiss' observations. For example, the "Rent-a-Judge" device, while resembling arbitration (the parties choose their own judge and, if there is no appeal, they retain the advantages of privacy), nevertheless assumes many of the essential features of an ordinary trial if a party does choose to appeal the judgment of the "rented" judge. While it is by no means certain that the appeal will be granted, in those cases in which it is, the findings of fact and, most important, the conclusions of law that had been reached by the "rented" judge will be reviewed by a court. In such instances, it can be argued, there is less reason than in other situations to be concerned about bypassing "public officials chosen by a process in which the public participates whose duty is "to explicate and give force to the values embodied in authoritative texts such as the Constitution and statutes: to interpret those values and to bring reality into accord with them."

Another distinction lies in the arbitration of disputes over interpretation and application of collective bargaining agreements. It has often been noted that the labor agreement is a species of state-authorized private legislation governing the terms and conditions of employment. Although American law limits what the parties can agree to in such contracts, it does encourage party autonomy. The entrustment of the adjudicatory function to private arbitrators mutually chosen by the parties is an integral part of the industrial self-government system established by such agreements. The extent to which the dispute resolution process selected by the parties should be overseen by the regular courts is thus a complex and delicate matter, aspects of which are examined in Chapter Eleven, Section H, Subsection 6 of the Casebook, dealing with judicial review of arbitration awards.

<u>Note 3</u> (Page 32): Would the publication of settlements enhance their "norm-setting" potential? A preliminary question is whether the prospect of publishing settlements would inhibit parties from reaching them in the first place? Among possible reasons for answering this question in the affirmative are: 1) Parties will often settle particular disputes on less favorable terms than they believe they are entitled to because, at the time, their desire to avoid litigation is compelling. Yet, if a similar dispute were to arise in the future, they might want to assert their claims to the fullest. Although the earlier settlement of a separate and distinct claim would not necessarily bind them, they might believe that its publication would put them at a disadvantage in resolving any future claim. 2) Related to the above, especially if the matter has been settled before a court action has been filed, privacy considerations often militate against publishing the terms of the settlement. Consider the case of a company that is alleged to have manufactured a product that injured a customer. If the customer's claim is settled

without publicity, the manufacturer may not have to confront any similar claims in the future. If the settlement terms are published, however, this might serve to: a) alert other users of the product to its potential dangers; and b) inform them that cash settlements can be procured. This is likely to multiply the number of claims that the manufacturer would have to face.

These possible reasons for why a party or parties might want to avoid publishing settlements lend further weight to Professor Fiss' observations about settlement's negative aspects. Had the above-described liability case gone to trial, it might have resulted in a judicial determination that the product was defective in presenting a risk of bodily harm or death to third persons. Under prevailing principles of collateral estoppel, the manufacturer would have been bound by that finding in subsequent litigation. By contrast, although the private, unpublicized settlement of the original claimant's claims would presumably have satisfied the claimant it would not have resulted in an authoritative, binding judicial determination of the manufacturer's basic liability. [It should be noted that, had the manufacturer prevailed at trial, other claimants would not have been bound by that determination because they were not parties to that action. By contrast, in jurisdictions that have eliminated the former requirement of mutuality of estoppel, new claimants could successfully invoke collateral estoppel to assert the finding of defective manufacture against the manufacturer.]

Even if parties were not inhibited in reaching settlements by the prospect of their being published, would such publication have the "norm-setting" potential suggested by the report. The term "norm-setting," is ambiguous. Is the Panel suggesting that published settlements would help similarly situated disputing parties to determine the appropriate terms for settling their own conflict? Or is it suggesting that courts would be influenced by such settlements? If the latter, would this be reconcilable with the anti-hearsay rule? Are settlements admissions against self interest? Don't most, if not all settlements, contain "boiler-plate" language to the effect that no liability is being admitted?

If only future disputants, and not courts, are contemplated, will Defendant Company's settlement of Claimant A's claim for $15,000 dispose of the question of the economic value of Claimant B's loss? Notwithstanding the potentially inhibitory effects of publishing settlements, does publication of Defendant Company's settlement of Claimant A's claim necessarily mean that it will not vigorously resist Claimant B's allegations of liability as well as damages?

<u>Note 4</u> (Page 32): In certain respects, ardent ADR advocates are strange political bedfellows. People do not necessarily act on their political ideologies, however, with respect to every public issue. Several facts about American judicial dispute-resolution mechanisms are clear. They are expensive, time-consuming and complex--and parties who participate in them are often disillusioned. These shortcomings strongly suggest the need for reform, regardless of one's basic political biases.

To be sure, the "expense" factor (which cannot be totally separated from the factors of complexity and delay in judicial proceedings) weighs less heavily upon the rich and, perhaps, the indigent (despite decreasing levels of government-supported free legal services) than it does upon the vast American middle-class. The latter, it has often been noted, cannot afford adequate legal services. Moreover, the middle-class, which is probably the most politically heterogeneous in American society, consists of large numbers of "liberals" as well as "conservatives." From a political perspective, therefore, the current interest in ADR may reflect nothing more ideological or sinister than dissatisfaction with judicial dispute resolution mechanisms, influenced to a large extent by the resulting economic hardships suffered by the largest and, perhaps, the most influential, social class in American society.

If Professor Abel is correct in concluding that the movement for "informal justice" contributes to "state repression and capitalist exploitation" but also has a "potential for liberation," should liberals (or conservatives) support it or oppose it?

<u>C. LAW AND ITS DISCONTENTS: A CRITICAL LOOK AT OUR LEGAL SYSTEM</u> (Page 33)

Many of the ideas expressed in President Bok's article (including the parts that are omitted here) have been incorporated in the "Paths to Justice" report examined above. In the part that is included in the Casebook, several of his points can be profitably explored. For example, he states: "Professors spend vast amounts of time examining the decisions of appellate courts, but make little effort to explore new voluntary mechanisms that might enable parties to resolve various types of disputes without going to court in the first place."

Query: Is the examination of appellate court decisions inconsistent with an exploration of those new voluntary mechanisms? Although skills training in voluntary mechanisms is highly desirable, are not the legal and policy issues underlying their use also important? For example, suppose a lawyer, who has been effectively trained in negotiation techniques or has intuitively understood them, negotiates a favorable settlement for his or her client. Is it not indispensable for that lawyer to know that the use of certain threats to induce the settlement may not only undermine the settlement, but can expose the lawyer to criminal liability for extortion? Or that the settlement can be rescinded if the lawyer withheld vital information from the party (or his or her attorney) with whom the lawyer negotiated the settlement? Yet these principles have been established in appellate court decisions. Learning about them and being able to critically appraise them would appear to be crucial to the effective use of negotiation techniques, among other ADR mechanisms.

Another point made by President Bok, which is also made in the "Paths to Justice" report and in the article by Professor Galanter discussed in the Notes following the Bok article, is that the number of litigated cases measured against population growth has not risen rapidly. The problem of court congestion appears to be attributable primarily to the increasing complexity of litigation. Whatever the causes, however, the fact of court congestion is real. Like the expense factor, this has also generated much support for the ADR movement.

<u>NOTES AND PROBLEMS FOR DISCUSSION</u> (Page 36)

<u>Note 1</u> (Page 36): Because of Japan's recent economic successes, Americans, it is often suggested, can learn much from that country about industrial organization, labor-management relations, and the appropriate role of government in economic development. Not surprisingly, the dramatic difference in the number of attorneys in Japan and the United States is frequently noted, and is especially emphasized in President Bok's article.

Several preliminary observations are in order. First, Japan's population is approximately one-half that of the United States'. Second, there are more than 600,000 attorneys in the United States, with California attorneys alone exceeding 80,000. Third, depending upon how you count them, attorneys in Japan number somewhere between 12,000 and 15,000. Fourth, Japan has the world's third largest annual gross national product, after the United States and the Soviet Union.

(The positions of Japan and the Soviet Union would probably be reversed if the Japanese yen were valued at a more realistic rate.) In any event, it is a highly developed, complex industrialized nation.

Aside from the questions posed in the Casebook, several others might be profitably explored. One is whether lack of Bar certification in the United States should necessarily prevent a person who has been trained in the law from engaging in any or all of the tasks that are performed by non-lawyers in Japan: e.g., "in-house legal advisors, judicial scriveners, administrative scriveners, patent attorneys, tax attorneys, and so forth." Another is whether, in view of what some have described as a "glut" of attorneys in the United States, re-thinking the fundamental goals of American legal education might not be in order. Should American law schools be transformed into training grounds not only for lawyers, but for members of other professions, such as journalists, civil service functionaries, business and labor union executives? Law schools in Japan and the European countries upon whose legal educational systems the Japanese system is modelled perform this role. Of course, law school education in Japan and those countries is undergraduate education. What, if anything, would prevent American law schools, which are post-graduate institutions, from seeking to implement similar goals? Since graduates who did not become lawyers after graduation would be precluded from engaging in ordinary litigation, would such a redirection of American law schools' goals ultimately develop greater reliance on non-litigative dispute resolution mechanisms? Or would it infect those who were not intending to become lawyers with a predeliction for judicial dispute resolution techniques? How would the answers to these questions differ if American law schools were to introduce significant blocks of ADR-related courses into their curricula?

CHAPTER TWO
NEGOTIATIONS

A. INTRODUCTION (Page 39)

Even under the National Labor Relations Act, an employer is required to engage in "rights" or "grievance" negotiations with its employees' bargaining representative; and the bargaining representative (the union) has a similar duty to negotiate grievances with the employer. That duty stems from Sections 8(a)(5) and 8(b)(3) of the NLRA. Thus, an employer's refusal to give a union information that it needs in deciding whether to pursue an employee's grievance is a "refusal to bargain" that violates Section 8(a)(5). See National Labor Relations Board v. Acme Industrial Co., 385 U.S. 432, 87 S.Ct. 565, 17 L.Ed.2d 495 (1967).

B. POWER VERSUS REASON (Page 41)

NLRB v. INSURANCE AGENTS' INT'L UNION (Page 41)

Why include this case here? One reason is that many cases in the Casebook involve various facets of American Labor Law. Most students and many professors will have had no previous experience in this area. It is therefore desirable to acquaint them as early as possible with some basic labor law principles. The case and Note 1 following it serve in part to acquaint the reader with the general outline of American labor law doctrine.

A more important reason for including Insurance Agents' here is that alternative dispute resolution mechanisms have a long and elaborate history in the area of labor law. Principles and techniques of negotiations ("interests" and "rights"), conciliation, mediation, fact-finding and arbitration are highly developed in labor-management relations. Because it is governed by special legislation, labor law differs from most of the other legal fields examined in the Casebook. Still, much of the accumulated labor law experience with ADR methods is transferable to other areas of legal regulation.

Perhaps the most important reason for including Insurance Agents' here is that it represents the rare occasion in which the Supreme Court examines the issue of "power versus reason" as applied to negotiations. To be sure, this discussion occurs in the context of a labor law case, an area in which Congress in NLRA Sections 7 and 13 has conferred special protection upon the right of employees to strike (i.e., to exert economic power) in aid of their negotiating positions. Yet, as will be more fully developed in the discussion of Note 4 following Insurance Agents', a strong argument can be made that the same factors are present in any type of negotiation.

Insurance Agents' examines not only the general duty that is imposed by the NLRA upon employers and unions to bargain about wages, hours and working conditions, but the Act's requirement that the bargaining be conducted in "good faith." The Court concludes that the NLRB had erred in holding that the union's mere use of an unorthodox type of economic pressure (power?) was a per se violation of the good-faith bargaining requirement. Although, as a general rule, neither statutory nor common law principles require disputing parties, outside the labor law field, to negotiate with one another at all, negotiated settlements, which constitute contracts, can be set aside on grounds of fraud in their inducement if a party had engaged in certain types of improper conduct during the negotiations.

NOTES AND PROBLEMS FOR DISCUSSION (Page 55)

Note 1 (Page 55): This note has proved to be helpful to those ADR students (a decided majority) who had not previously taken a course in Labor Law.

Note 2 (Page 57): The answer to this question is clearly "interests" negotiations. The union and employer were not trying to negotiate rights under an existing collective bargaining agreement. Rather, they were trying to negotiate the terms of an agreement, i.e., to decide what would go into it. Unlike most other types of "interests" negotiations, however, e.g., between buyers and sellers of property, the union and employer could not choose not to negotiate with one another over these matters; the statute compelled them to do so, and in good faith at that.

Note 3 (Page 57): As noted above, the principal case deals with "interests" negotiations and not "rights" negotiations. It is nevertheless useful to note that the language of NLRA Section 8(d) requiring the employer and union to "confer in good faith with respect to * * * the negotiation of an agreement, or any question arising thereunder * * *" is the statutory basis for the duty to bargain about "rights" or "grievances."

Note 4 (Page 57): A strong argument can be made for the proposition that "force" or "power" is an essential ingredient, i.e., a prime motive power, in any type of negotiation. Will not "informed persuasion," to use Professor Cox's phrase, operate only when negotiating parties are sufficiently convinced that the party with whom they are negotiating can exercise sufficient power to cause them harm?

If, for example, husband and wife negotiate support payments or a property division in connection with a marriage dissolution, won't their willingness to come to terms be greatly influenced by what they believe a court would order if the case went to trial--what some have described as negotiating "in the shadow of the law"? Does that not translate into "power" (actual or potential) of one party to persuade the court to order payments that are higher than the other party is willing to make? Or, conversely, the power of the other party to persuade the court to order lower payments than the opposing party is willing to accept? If husband and wife value their reputations for fairness and decency among mutual friends, won't their bargain be shaped in part by a desire not to destroy that reputation? Isn't the potential threat to that reputation, if their settlement terms are deemed unfair by people whose good opinions they value, another aspect of power in bargaining?

The role of power in other types of bargaining is equally apparent. When disputing nations negotiate with one another, isn't each influenced by its perception of the other's, and its own, military, political and economic strengths and weaknesses? Isn't the desire not to outrage world public opinion (the analogue to the divorcing couple's concern for their future reputation among their mutual friends), a major factor in determining what each nation is willing to settle for?

Note 5 (Page 57): In Dearborn Firefighters Union, Local No. 412, I.A.F.F.v. City of Dearborn, reported at p. 844 of the Casebook, the Michigan Supreme Court examines its own and other states' statutes that require public sector bargaining impasses to be arbitrated. These statutes implicitly recognize that, by depriving public employee unions of the strike weapon, the essential "motive power" for effective collective bargaining is removed. In a sense, however, the prospect of compulsory arbitration provides a new motive power. In theory at least, the terms that the public sector employer or the union will accept in negotiations will be greatly influenced by its perception of the other party's "power" to persuade the arbitrator to rule in its favor. Unions will also often defy a state's strike prohibition in hopes, often realized, that a negotiated agreement settling the economic issues will also include a general amnesty for the illegal strikers. Appeals to public opinion by the union (and the employer) are also part of the weaponry available to each side. At times, the public is persuaded that the public employer's economic proposals are unfair; and that the services provided by the public employees in question--teachers, sanitation department workers, police or firefighters--will deteriorate if those proposals are not improved. Because taxpayers, who make up a large part of the public, can be described as the ultimate public employers, they can often be persuaded by the nominal public employers that the union's demands are exorbitant; and that they, the taxpayers, will ultimately have to pay the bill if the union's demands are met.

Note 6(a) (Page 58): In view of Justice Brennan's language quoted in this Note, is it clear that the majority would have gone the same way if the union had engaged in acts of physical sabotage or violent behavior in its efforts to persuade the employer to accept its proposed contract terms? Arguably, such acts would inevitably infect the negotiations with ill will, thereby insuring their failure. An NLRB finding of a per se Section 8(b)(3) violation could therefore be said to rest "on some unique character of the union tactics involved." On the other hand, an equally strong argument can be made that, as long as the union negotiators sincerely sought to reach agreement, listening to and carefully appraising the employer's position, its resort to violence or physical sabotage, outside the bargaining room, should not, by itself, constitute an 8(b)(3) violation. Moreover, just as the employer in Insurance Agents' could have discharged the malingering employees without violating Sections 8(a)(1) and (3) of the Act, so could it have invoked the processes of the criminal law if the employees had engaged in acts of violence and physical sabotage.

Note 6(b) (Page 58): The analogy with war-time negotiations (without a cease-fire) is another vehicle for examining whether the union should be held to have committed a per se violation of its good-faith bargaining duty if it had resorted to violence. One might also pose the following question here. Suppose a husband and wife are negotiating a property settlement agreement in a divorce proceeding. To persuade his wife to accept his terms, the husband threatens to beat her if she does not. As a token of his earnest, he shoots her favorite cat while she watches. Frightened, she accedes to his terms. The agreement is incorporated in the divorce decree, but three months later the wife seeks to rescind the agreement, setting forth the facts as described above. Should the court grant rescission? As discussed on page 193 of the Casebook (Note 3, following Press Machinery Corporation v. Smith R.P.M. Corporation), in many states threats made in the course of negotiations may constitute the crime of extortion. Here the husband went beyond threats and actually engaged in violent conduct directed against the property (the cat) of the wife. Clearly, he would be punishable under the criminal law. It is also likely that the agreement could be rescinded on grounds of duress. In the labor relations field, however, the tactics engaged in by the union in Insurance Agents' constituted a form of economic duress, which the Court ruled was permitted by the NLRA. Had the union engaged in physical sabotage or violence, however, the duress would be of the kind that normally would permit rescission. The question remains, however, whether the factors discussed earlier, which reflect the policies of the NLRA, would limit the employer to seeking redress from the criminal justice system, but bind it to its collective bargaining agreement as long as the union otherwise negotiated in good faith.

ON MISSILES, DETERRENTS AND UNITED STATES-SOVIET UNION NEGOTIATIONS (Page 58)

These excerpts from the debates over the proposed nuclear freeze, MX missile development and Soviet-American negotiations are included to demonstrate some other problems that are implicated in the tension between "power" and "reason" in negotiations. Neither Senator Leahy nor Senator Hatfield appear to disagree with the President's basic assumption: that successful disarmament negotiations with the Soviet Union depend upon the ability of the United States to present convincing evidence of its own military strength. They all seem to share, therefore, a basic belief in the centrality of "power" in negotiations.

On a number of related issues, however, they differ with the President. The Senators believe that MX missile development is not needed to achieve the required level of military strength; that the expense of developing the missile is prohibitive; and that its development, rather than intimidating the Soviet Union into accepting terms that are favorable to the United States, will only provoke it to exert greater efforts to develop its own military capabilities. Their remarks underscore potential problems that can arise when total reliance is placed upon "power" in negotiations. Regardless of the type of negotiation involved--settling a personal injury claim, working out a marital property settlement, concluding a new collective bargaining agreement, arranging the sale or purchase of property (a single family residence or a multi-billion dollar multi-national corporation), settling boundary or other types of disputes between nations--these problems must be considered. Will the cost of achieving superior bargaining leverage exceed the benefits such a position might reasonably produce in negotiations? Will the display of power, rather than causing the other party to capitulate, merely strengthen that party's resolve to resist or to seek ways to increase its own bargaining strength? Is a party's effort to increase its bargaining power wasted because that party already enjoys equal or superior bargaining leverage?

Did the resumption of disarmament negotiations between the Soviet Union and the United States (after the Soviet Union had remained away from the bargaining table to protest American deployment of cruise missiles in western Europe), vindicate President Reagan's insistence upon a military build-up as a prerequisite to meaningful negotiations? Are sufficient facts available to answer that question intelligently? How would the President's promotion of the Strategic Defense Initiative (sometimes called the "Star Wars" program) fit into this area? With regard to the hijacking to Beirut of the TWA 747 in June, 1985, how indispensable to the ultimate release of the American passengers who were held hostage was the positioning of American war vessels off the Lebanese coast? Did that facilitate or hinder the hostages'release?

<u>NOTES AND PROBLEMS FOR DISCUSSION</u> (Page 65)

<u>Note 1</u> (Page 65): The questions raised in this Note are examined in the above discussion of "On Missiles, Deterrents and United States-Soviet Union Negotiations."

<u>Note 2</u> (Page 65): Like settlements of legal claims before or after suits are filed, the high settlement rate of labor disputes that are subject to arbitration, even when a union may not strike, probably reflects, more than anything else, the fact that the parties are bargaining "in the shadow of the law." The arbitrator, although not possessed of all the attributes of a judge, nevertheless exercises similar functions. The arbitrator's authority to make a final and binding determination of the dispute necessarily causes each party to be uncertain whether it will ultimately prevail. "Does the opposing party have the 'power' to persuade the arbitrator of the the rightness of its position?" The answer (real or imagined) to that question will greatly influence the willingness of a union or an employer to settle a grievance short of arbitration. Appeals to public opinion and the threat of strikes, despite their illegality, as discussed

above, can also play major roles in facilitating labor dispute settlements.

Note 3 (Page 66): At one end, the Susskind and Rubin definition represents the essence of the "power" rationale, at the other, the Menkel-Meadow definition the essence of the "reason" rationale. An argument can be made that negotiation can perform all the roles assigned to it by these authors. To what extent is one's perception of the nature of negotiation governed by reasoned analysis, as opposed to the nature of one's own personality?

Note 4 (Page 66): One might ask whether Professor Fisher's definitions of power are any more or less realistic than the suggestion made above that the "power" of an adversary to persuade a judge or arbitrator of the rightness of his or her position is a major factor in whether a negotiated settlement of a dispute will be reached.

Note 5 (Page 67): If A (Employer) is seeking to buy B's (Employee's) services, the price A is willing to pay will be greatly influenced by: 1) the ability of A to find others who will provide those services for less money; 2) the ability of B, through collective action with other employees of A, to inflict economic harm upon A if A does not pay what B regards as a fair price for B's services. Similarly, B's willingness to work at the price A is willing to pay will be greatly influenced by: 1) B's perception of A's ability to find others who will work at the same or a lower price; 2) B's ability to persuade other employees to engage in collective action. These factors, among others, play a significant role in determining the "worth" of services or dollars.

C. PROFESSIONAL RESPONSIBILITY (Page 68)

KATH v. WESTERN MEDIA, INC. (Page 68)

This case does not involve a disciplinary proceeding against appellees' Wyoming attorney. Rather, the appellants are allowed to rescind an agreement settling a law suit because, when they entered it, they were not informed of important facts that were known to opposing counsel. Although the court discusses the attorney's heightened ethical duty, it does not suggest that he should be subject to disciplinary proceedings. Should he be?

NOTES AND PROBLEMS FOR DISCUSSION (Page 73)

Note 1 (Page 73): Can it be reasonably argued that if a

law suit had not yet been filed, appellants would not have been prejudiced by not knowing about Planalp's role in the Montana litigation, since they would not have had Planalp's deposition to take into account? Would the attorney's duty to disclose be as compelling under those circumstances as it was after suit was filed? Conversely, even though a law suit had not yet been filed, don't the parties negotiate with at least a tacit understanding that, if negotiations fail, a law suit is always possible?

If no attorneys were involved in the Wyoming negotiations, the failure of the appellees themselves to disclose to the appellants that the Montana attorney knew that they intended to sue the appellees at a later date may have been insufficient to permit rescission of a settlement. (The court suggests that the attorney had a higher duty of candor in negotiations than his clients). If this is really the law in this area, does it not operate to deter people from seeking the assistance of counsel in negotiations?

These questions, and their possible answers, suggest some limits on the use of "power" in negotiations. Whether the witholding of the information would lead to the same result without regard to whether parties negotiate with or without attorneys, ethical principles having the force of law may limit what the parties may say, or conversey require them to reveal certain information that would be damaging to their position.

<u>Note 2</u> (Page 73): It would appear that Blackstone would be in violation of both the 1978 and 1983 standards. His letter necessarily relates to "evidence regarding the occurrence or transaction involved" as well as "his opinion as to the merits of the claim or defenses of a party," and therefore violates DR 3.6 of the ABA's 1978 Model Code. As for Rule 3.6 of the ABA's Model Rules, Blackstone has made an extrajudicial statement, and he "reasonably should know that it will have a substantial likelihood of materially prejudicing an adjudicative proceeding."

<u>Note 3</u> (Page 75): Blackstone's insistence upon a $100,000 settlement when he knows that he and his client are willing to settle for $50,000 raises several problems. First, he is likely to be in violation of E.C. [Ethical Consideration] 7-7 of the ABA's Model Code of Professional Responsibility if he made this demand without his client's approval. Second, even if his client approved, the insurance company might "call his bluff," and simply refuse to make any offer, or make one that was less than the $50,000 he and his client

were actually willing to accept. The more fundamental problem, however, is whether this "puffing" in negotiations--if one assumes that both attorney and client agree on the strategy--constitutes a failure to "act honestly and in good faith." Although, on the face of it, the attorney would appear to be engaging in positive acts of misrepresentation, his words and conduct cannot be isolated from the general practice of negotiations. It would not be unreasonable for him to assume that, if he offers to settle the case for $50,000, the insurance company would be convinced that he was really prepared to settle for a substantially lower amount. His duty to his client, therefore, might require him to insist upon a figure that was higher than what he was prepared to settle for. In view of this long-standing negotiation technique, a strong argument can be made the attorney commits no ethical violation when he acts this way.

CHAPTER THREE
CONCILIATION

A. INTRODUCTION (Page 77)

It may be appropriate here to explore the attributes of a good conciliator. Among these are patience; self-confidence; ability to express oneself clearly; intelligence (reflected in the ability to understand the nature of the issues dividing the parties, or to prod the parties into articulating those issues clearly); tact; a sense, intuitive or born of experience, as to when negotiations ought to be suspended, when later negotiating sessions ought to be scheduled, and where to hold them. Above all, a good conciliator must have integrity and intellectual honesty. While these are indispensable traits under all circumstances, they are especially important if the parties have difficulty dealing with one another directly. Under such circumstances, for conciliation to succeed, the parties must trust the conciliator to reveal only those articulated positions to the opposing party that they have authorized the conciliator to reveal, and not to misrepresent one party's proposals to the other.

B. MARRIAGE DISSOLUTION (Page 79)

IN RE MARRIAGE OF PENNEY (Page 79)

This case is an example of compulsory conciliation. Compulsory conciliation, which reminds one of the old adage about "bringing a horse to water but not being able to make it drink," has severe limitations. However, what might induce disputing parties to seek the aid of a conciliator voluntarily? If the parties can't resolve their underlying dispute, why would they agree to have a third party neutral assist them in resolving it? There are several possible answers to these questions. The main one is that, though the parties can not resolve their underlying dispute, they may recognize that they have had difficulty communicating with one another about it--and that if the channels of communication are opened, a way to a resolution may be found. Another is that although in theory conciliators (in contrast to mediators) should not propose particular ways of resolving disputes, many, if not most, conciliators do so. Disputing parties may agree to a conciliator's intervention in hopes that the latter will suggest a mutually acceptable resolution to the impasse. Finally, many parties realize that, although they are having difficulty resolving their dispute, relying upon a judicial proceeding to do so may be unsatisfactory because of the problems of expense, delay, complexity and heightened adversariness examined previously. Avoiding those problems may be a sufficient reason for enlisting the aid of a third party neutral conciliator, even though they have had difficulty resolving their own dispute.

NOTES AND PROBLEMS FOR DISCUSSION (Page 81)

Note 1 (Page 81): An argument can be made that compulsory conciliation is equally appropriate (or inappropriate) in states with "marital-breakdown" grounds for marriage dissolution as in those with traditional fault grounds for divorce. The main purpose of the movement toward "no fault" marriage dissolution was to eliminate the rancor and airing of "dirty linen" in the courtroom that were associated with the traditional fault bases for divorce. In either case, however, the underlying reasons for the apparent breakdown of a marriage are the same.

Note 2 (Page 81): Aside from avoiding the potential constitutional questions, there are good reasons for the court to grant the request of the spouse who petitioned for the divorce that the conciliator be a non-clerical private marriage counselor. One is that if the marriage is to be salvaged, the petitioning spouse must change his or her mind about seeking the dissolution in the first place. If that spouse strongly objects to the "type" of conciliator preferred by the other, chances for effecting a reconciliation will be slim. As for the constitutional questions, it should be noted first that the statute itself provides that "clergymen" are among those eligible to serve as conciliators. The constitutional problems are less serious if the parties mutually agree that a "clergyman" should serve as their conciliator, since the decision is then the parties' rather than the court's. If one of the spouses (or both) objects to naming a clergyman, however, the court's designation of one as conciliator would seem to violate the First Amendment's "establishment of religion" and "free exercise" clauses under the reasoning of the Supreme Court in the recent church-state separation cases. See Grand Rapids School District v. Ball, ___ U.S. ___, 105 S.Ct. 3216, ___ L.Ed.2d ___ (1985).

Note 3 (Page 81): A preliminary question is whether there is a constitutional right to have an unsatisfactory marriage dissolved. The Supreme Court held in Boddie v. Connecticut, 401 U.S. 371, 91 S.Ct. 780, 28 L.Ed.2d 113 (1971) that the failure of a state to waive filing and service-of-process fees for an indigent divorce petitioner was a discriminatory denial of access to the courts, and thereby violated Fourteenth Amendment due process. The Court did not hold that the right to a divorce was constitutionally guaranteed. Even if such a constitutional right does not exist, however, the rationale of Boddie could be applied if a court indefinitely delays hearing a divorce petition pending the conclusion of conciliation efforts. Arguably, at some point, the conciliation will have gone on long enough force a conclusion that it will bear no fruit. For the court to insist that conciliation efforts continue would constitute arbitrary action in violation of due process guarantees.

Note 4 (Page 82): As indicated by the misgivings expressed by the court itself in Penney, compulsory conciliation of marital disputes is not likely to be very productive under the circumstances of that case: the parties having unsuccessfully attempted conciliation before the dissolution proceeding was filed, and the petitioning spouse strongly objecting to conciliation. Even where conciliation has not been attempted previously, there is serious question about a mandatory conciliation requirement in divorce cases, as well as in other types of cases. Although in some states, statistics indicate that some marriages may be "patched up" by conciliation, they also indicate that the parties are likely to resume their efforts to dissolve the marriage in the future.

Note 5 (Page 82): In re Marriage of Ried held that the allegations in the husband's answer did not constitute a request for conciliation as contemplated by the statute. In effect, they merely presented a factual question to be decided by the court, namely whether the marriage had failed.

CHAPTER FOUR
MEDIATION

A. INTRODUCTION (Page 83)

This section is largely informational and does not require extensive classroom elaboration.

B. COMMUNITY DISPUTES (Page 86)

GORDON v. FAY (Page 86)

How might the Massachussetts procedures, including referral to mediation, for handling misdemeanor complaints and those issued by the Housing Court be more satisfactory to society in general and to the individuals involved than ordinary criminal law processes? From the complaining party's viewpoint, being made whole for injuries incurred as a result of the defendant's conduct, and preventing similar conduct of the defendant in the future, are usually more important goals than retribution. If mediation can achieve such goals, the complaining party gains much more than he or she would in an ordinary criminal proceeding--although it is not unusual for a convicted defendant to be placed on probation on condition that the defendant make restitution. From the defendant's viewpoint, there is no official record of the issuance of a criminal complaint. Moreover, the defendant might persuade the complaining party in the course of mediation that no misdemeanor or other violation was committed, thereby terminating the dispute without recourse to a criminal trial. As for society's gains, it is, first of all, spared the expense, time and effort that would be normally consumed in a contested criminal proceeding. In addition, depending upon the outcome of the mediation, the ranks of convicted criminals might not increase.

Recall, however, Professor Fiss' admonition about settlement of civil suits and his allusions to plea bargaining in the criminal context. Is there a danger in the Massachusetts procedure that people who should be tainted with a criminal conviction will evade that punishment? Will the parties be able to make intelligent choices during the mediation? Or, will they, in order to avoid the criminal taint, confess guilt even though there is a strong likelihood that they would have been found innocent had they gone to trial?

NOTES AND PROBLEMS FOR DISCUSSION (Page 91)

Note 1 (Page 91): The questions raised in this Note are

a continuation of those examined in the above comments on Gordon v. Fay. Notwithstanding the traditional definition of crimes as offenses against the sovereign, in practice the criminal law tacitly--and sometimes not so tacitly--recognizes that it is an alternate vehicle for providing relief to persons injured by another's criminal acts. In that context, the mediation process, as well as the dismissal of charges upon the defendant correcting the violation, would fit comfortably into these special goals of the criminal law.

Note 2 (Page 92): The process described by Dean Snyder, in which judges "tend to bargain directly with a defendant in court" would appear to be more appropriately denominated as "negotiation" rather than "mediation."

Note 3 (Page 93): The implications of Professor Fuller's observations fit neatly into those made more expressly by Professor Fiss. The settlement of the criminal case by mediation, with the resultant failure to issue a criminal complaint, creates the theoretical possibility that the procedure may create a gap in the legal rules governing the situation that gave rise to the proceeding. "Theoretical" only, in that in most situations the law on the subject will be abundantly clear, either because the statute is clear on its face or the court interpretations of it in contested cases leave no doubt as to its meaning. At the same time, the social and individual goals described in the above comments on Gordon v. Fay may make the mediation alternative attractive in many cases.

C. CUSTODY AND VISITATION DISPUTES

McLAUGHLIN v. SUPERIOR COURT FOR THE COUNTY OF SAN MATEO (Page 93)

The most important feature of the California legislation is its mandatory character. The statute requires contested custody or visitation matters to be preceded by a mediation session. As a general rule, voluntary mediation is to be preferred, and is likely to be more effective than, mandatory mediation. Nevertheless, the prospects for successful mediation, though mandatory, with regard to custody and visitation disputes are higher than in some other areas. In important respects, the relationship between a husband and wife who are seeking to dissolve their marriage and who have children is similar to the relationship between a union and employer who have a labor dispute. In both cases, the parties will not sever their ties once the dispute is resolved. They continue to be bound to one another in an ongoing relationship. The union and employer must still deal with one another in future contract negotiations and in the day-to-day administration of existing contracts. The former spouses maintain contact through their relationship with their children and through any post-marital support obligations running between them. Under such circumstances, a dispute resolution devised by the parties themselves is more likely to be respected than one that is imposed upon them by an outside authority.

As indicated by the Notes following the case, which are discussed below, the California statute raises other problems that have not been cured by McLaughlin.

NOTES AND PROBLEMS FOR DISCUSSION (Page 100)

Note 1 (Page 100): The principal problem in the California legislation is that, by authorizing the "mediator" to recommend a custody and visitation disposition to the court, the statute inevitably undermines the "mediator's" potential for inducing the parties to arrive at their own agreement on these issues. In a sense, requiring that the "mediator" be subjected to cross-examination, if (s)he makes a recommendation to the court, merely compounds the problem. An indispensable element of a successful mediation is that the disputing parties be candid and open with one another. Among other ways, this is reflected in the statute's requirement of confidentiality. If the parties know, however, that the mediator can make a recommendation to the court based on their confidential discussions, the parties will necessarily be less than frank with one another in the mediation sessions. That the mediator who makes such a recommendation is subject to cross-examination does not alleviate this problem, since the stifling effect on the mediation sessions will still be felt. It is probably fair to say that, though denominated a "mediator" by the statute, the "mediator's" function, because of the power to make recommendations to the court, is closer to that of a fact-finder. As a result, if a court were to permit the mediator to make recommendations when the parties could not resolve these issues with the mediator's aid, the statute's effectiveness would be severely limited, if not totally destroyed. Significantly, most, if not all, California courts have adopted local rules prohibiting the mediator from making such recommendations.

Note 2 (Page 100): International Ass'n of Machinists, etc. v. National Mediation Board was an action to compel the National Mediation Board to proffer arbitration under the Railway Labor Act. The D.C. Circuit held, among other things, that the federal district court had improperly called on

Board members to give their reasons for not profferring arbitration, and that it had improperly struck Board interrogations in view of its failure to respond.

In Tomlinson of High Point, Inc., the NLRB, in an unfair labor practice proceeding, rejected an effort to subpoena a conciliator from the Federal Mediation and Conciliation Service who had tried to assist the parties to resolve their bargaining impasse. Stated the Board: "However useful the testimony of a conciliator might be to the Board in any given case, we can appreciate the strong considerations of public policy underlying the [FMCS] regulation and the refusal to make exceptions to it because of the unique position which the conciliators occupy. To execute successfully their function of assisting in the settlement of labor disputes, the conciliators must maintain a reputation for impartiality, and the parties to conciliation conferences must feel free to talk without any fear that the concilator may subsequently make disclosures as a witness in some other proceeding, to the possible disadvantage of a party to the conference. If conciliators were permitted or required to testify about their activities, or if the production of notes or reports of their activities could be required, not even the strictest adherence to purely factual matters would prevent the evidence from favoring or seeming to favor one side or the other. The inevitable result would be that the usefulness of the Conciliation Service in the settlement of future disputes would be seriously impaired, if not destroyed. The resultant injury to the public interest would clearly outweigh the benefit to be derived from making their testimony available in particular cases." 74 N.L.R.B. at 685.

Note 3 (Page 100): Professors Folberg and Taylor suggest that if the mediator is cross-examined "the adversely affected party doing the questioning could be held to have waived the objections to the revelations made by the mediator in court."

Note 4 (Page 101): Could the court appoint a member of the clergy? If it did so, would the constitituional problem be more acute than if it appointed that same person as a conciliator, since the California statute authorizes the "mediator" to make custody and visitation recommendations to the court? Would constitutional problems arise if a judge appointed his or her brother-in-law as mediator, or the taxicab driver who had driven the judge to work that morning and had seemed to have an abundance of common sense and a pleasant personality?

A major problem concerning licensure and educational standards for mediators is that there is no general agreement as to precisely what training and background will guarantee that a person will function effectively as a mediator. Mediation has been effective in labor relations in the past, for example, despite the absence of any licensing requirements for those who serve in such a capacity. The backgrounds of private divorce mediators have also been varied, and many have been successful in their work. At the same time, as the ADR movement expands, there is much potential for abuse by persons purporting to be qualified mediators. The vague wording of the ABA Standards would appear to reflect the general uncertainty as to the precise qualifications for a mediator. Ultimately, however, this problem will have to be addressed, although its eventual solution will surely not please everyone interested or involved in ADR.

Regarding the similarity of labor and divorce mediators' skills and functions, Markowitz and Engram note: "[W]e already employ many techniques in common: reducing expectations, pointing out the consequences of failure, ordering priorities, focusing on problems rather than on personalities, suggesting compromises, and face-saving."

D. PROFESSIONAL RESPONSIBILITY PROBLEMS (Page 102)

LANGE v. MARSHALL (Page 102)

Could one ever prove that, but for a mediator's failure to carry out his or her responsibilities, the parties' bargain would have been more favorable to the plaintiff?

NOTES AND PROBLEMS FOR DISCUSSION (Page 104)

Note 1 (Page 104): Proving damages, as noted above, will be difficult. Even if damages are proved, tenable arguments can be made for and against mediator liability in such circumstances. The question requires a definition of the mediator's role, and of what is the best deal for disputing parties. Is it to gain the most for each party in dollars and cents, or to facilitate the conclusion of an agreement that each party will be comfortable with and whose implementation will be reasonably assured? If the first definition of a "best deal" is adopted, it can be argued that the failure of a mediator to advise the parties of the risks of mediation and the availability of other dispute resolving mechanisms, including litigation, amounts to malpractice. Adoption of the second definition, however, would arguably lead to an opposite result. Note that Section I.A of the Standards of

Practice for Lawyer Mediators in Family Disputes, adopted by the American Bar Association in 1984 (see p. 927 of the Casebook) provides in part that "[t]he mediator shall define the process in context so that the participants understand the differences between mediation and other means of conflict resolution available to them."

The non-attorney mediator should employ an attorney to draft a settlement agreement in legal form to avoid liability for the unauthorized practice of law.

Canon 5 states: "A Lawyer Should Exercise Independent Judgment on Behalf of a Client." At the same time, Ethical Considerations 5-15 provides, in part, that "there are many instances in which a lawyer may properly serve multiple clients having potentially differing interests in matters not involving litigation." Professor Linda Silberman, in the article cited in the Casebook, notes that, although the traditional attitude of Bar Associations and the Courts has been that attorneys violate Canon 5 if they serve both husband and wife in the preparation of a divorce settlement agreement, some cases have allowed lawyers to do this.

As for the issue posed in the last sentence of this question, see the discussion of Note 4 below.

Note 2 (Page 105): See Section I.G of the ABA's Standards for Lawyer Mediators, etc. (page 927 of the Casebook), discussed in the next Note. See also, Section IV A (page ___ of the Casebook) which provides: "The mediator shall assure that there is full financial disclosure, evaluation and development of relevant factual information in the mediation process, such as each would reasonably receive in the discovery process, or that the parties have sufficient information to intelligently waive the right to such disclosure."

Note 3 (Page 105): Advantages of a lawyer mediator: familiarity with legal principles might serve to alert both parties to possible pitfalls; same person who mediated would prepare the settlement agreement in legal terms, thereby minimizing the risk of insufficient communication between the non-lawyer mediator and the lawyer who drafted the agreement. Advantages of a non-lawyer mediator: may have a better background in the behavioral sciences, and therefore better trained in the art and skills of mediation.

Note 4 (Page 105): At page 76 of their cited article, Markowitz and Engram state: "In labor negotiations, the parties' experience, the availability of traditional economic sanctions, and the use of professional representatives all militate against mediators' judging the fairness of the bargain struck. Instead, they should be oriented solely toward obtaining a settlement, and they should avoid intruding on whatever the parties deem to be mutually acceptable. The divorce mediator should not be so cavalier. A 'bad' divorce cannot be blamed on careless representatives. More important divorce agreements are not likely to be renegotiated within two or three years or to be ameliorated by benign contract administration or constructive grievance handling. The divorce mediator also has an ethical obligation to consider the children, who may be unwitting victims of their parents' discord."

WERLE v. RHODE ISLAND BAR ASSOCIATION (Page 105)

NOTES AND PROBLEMS FOR DISCUSSION (Page 111):

Note 1 (Page 111): The First Circuit does not decide whether Werle was engaged in the unauthorized practice of law. It merely holds that, even if he was not, the conduct of the Rhode Island Bar Association was privileged under the circumstances, even if that conduct could properly be characterized as state action, which is another question not decided by the court. Nevertheless, in some of its language the court strongly suggests that Werle was in fact engaged in the unauthorized practice of law, as defined by the Rhode Island statutes. Would such a holding, if widely followed, toll the death knell for divorce mediation? Or would it merely limit the type of advertising that divorce mediators could distribute? Could Werle have retained an attorney to perform the services described in the brochure, as long as he did not advertise that he would do so? Did Werle advertise that he would procure or aid in procuring a divorce? Shouldn't the normal duties of a divorce mediator include exploring the possibilities of reconciliation with the parties?

Note 2 (Page 111): It is ironic that Dr. Werle, a professional mediator dedicated to providing an alternative to judicial judicial dispute resolution, invoked the aid of the federal court to settle his dispute with the Rhode Island Bar Association. He may have sought to mediate the dispute but was unable to procure the Bar Association's agreement to do so; the court's opinion is silent on this. Under the circumstances, even if he had suggested mediation to the Bar Association, it would have refused. Even if the dispute had been mediated, it would have resulted at best in a settlement of the individual differences between Dr. Werle and the Bar Association. However, no principles would emerge from such a settlement that would guide either the Rhode Island Bar Association, other Bar Associations or other mediators with respect to their future conduct. Another example of the shortcomings of settlements, negotiated with or without the aid of third parties, suggested by Professor Fiss.

CHAPTER FIVE
FACTFINDING

A. INTRODUCTION (Page 112)

B. PUBLIC EMPLOYMENT (Page 114)

WASCO COUNTY v. AFSCME, LOCAL 2752 (Page 114)

The problem in this case is a variation of the one posed in *Insurance Agents'*, reported at Page 41 of the Casebook. In that case, the United States Supreme Court had to decide whether the employee's "slowdown" during negotiations constituted a per se refusal of the union to bargain in good faith under the NLRA. Here, the Oregon Board and Supreme Court must determine whether an employer who (after a bargaining impasse has been reached but before the state's impasse resolving procedures, including factfinding, have been exhausted), grants a wage increase in an amount previously offered to and rejected by the union, commits a per se refusal to bargain. The problem arises because of decisions under the NLRA making it clear that an employer's unilateral wage increase while that subject is under negotiation normally represents an unlawful refusal to bargain with the employee's designated bargaining representative. See, e.g., NLRB v. Katz, 369 U.S. 736, 82 S.Ct. 1107, 8 L.Ed.2d 230 (1962). After an impasse is reached in negotiations, however, an employer does not violate the NLRA if it institutes "by unilateral action changes which are in line with or which are no more favorable than" those it offered before impasse. Bi-Rite Foods, Inc., 147 N.L.R.B. 59 (1964). The problem in *Wasco* stems from the state's requirement of factfinding as part of the negotiating process in the public sector. Essentially, the question is whether, despite the apparent impasse, only when the impasse-resolving procedures, including factfinding, have been completed, can there said to be a genuine impasse. If that is so, a unilateral wage increase by the employer during this period is a refusal to bargain in good faith. Although not expressed in precisely these terms, this is essentially the position adopted in *"Wasco II"*, discussed in Note 1 following the principal case.

Another question stemming from *"Wasco I"* is whether the type of problem examined in that case can arise when factfinding is employed outside the labor relations field, such as in the next case, Jeffery v. Weintraub. It is very unlikely to arise there for a number of reasons. One is that if an impasse has been reached in bargaining between parties outside the field of labor relations, and they have chosen to resort to factfinding, any unilateral change would represent a new concession on the part of the party making it. By contrast, in labor negotiations when an employer institutes a unilateral wage increase after a bargaining impasse has been reached, it does not represent a new concession, since the wage increase is limited to what the employer had previously offered and the union had refused. In addition, in contrast to the statutory duty of an employer to negotiate in good faith with the employees' designated bargaining representative, no such duty to negotiate normally applies to people outside the labor relations field.

NOTES AND PROBLEMS FOR DISCUSSION (Page 118)

Note 1 (Page 118): See discussion of "Wasco I" above.

Note 3 (Page 120): A factfinder's report, especially in the labor relations field, will often justify a public employer's or a public employee union's agreeing to a deal that might otherwise displease its constitutents--taxpayers on the one hand, union members on the other. Not infrequently, a union's leaders, more conscious of a public employer's predicament than are its members, may be more willing than the members to accept a low wage offer. Under such circumstances, the factfinder's report may be determinative, since it indicates to the members what a qualified neutral party believes is a fair resolution of the impasse. Similarly, a public employer may in a given set of negotiations be willing to grant the union's wage demands, but it fears the voters' reaction if it does so. Here too the factfinder's report may make the desired solution more palatable to the latter. This function of factfinding may explain the apparent dearth of communication from the public to the public employer following the issuance of a factfinder's report.

C. PRIVATE DISPUTES

JEFFERY v. WEINTRAUB (Page 120)

The absence of express language making factfinding here "advisory only," such as is present in the educational employment relations act, arguably suggests an intent to make it binding. This implication is clearly rebutted, however, by the legislative history (the council chairman's remarks set forth in footnote 4) and by the provision of the ordinance that expressly permits the parties to request the factfinder to "serve as an arbitrator [and] to finally determine the dispute concerning moorage fees * * * ."

NOTES AND PROBLEMS FOR DISCUSSION (Page 126)

Note 2 (Page 126): Unlike the public employer in "Wasco I", the landlord is engaged in a profit-making enterprise. That a proposed rent increase is "unreasonable" is not likely to deflect many landlords from their goal of realizing a maximum profit on the rental of their property. Even if the rent is unreasonably high, a landlord would have a strong interest in charging that amount, as long as enough tenants could be found who would pay the landlord's price. *A fortiori*, notwithstanding a factfinder's determination that a particular rent increase was "unreasonable," most landlords would not find it hard to insist upon it if it were "less than the corresponding rise in the Consumer Price Index for the same period." As for the direct rent control feature of the ordinance, note the language in Section 7 (set forth in footnote 2): "No contested moorage fee increase shall take effect until the conclusion of fact-finding proceedings; provided that the moorage owner or operator may recover retroactively such increases as are found reasonable by the fact-finder."

Note 3 (Page 126): In a certain sense, the term "moral suasion" in this context really is a euphemism for "a potential threat of future economic or political harm." In the public employment sector, a public employer may fear ultimate retaliation by the voters if it disregards the factfinder's recommendations; a union may also fear that if it disregards those recommendations because they are contrary to its bargaining position, the public employer's resolve to resist the union's demands will be stiffened by the recommendations. In the private sector, as in Jeffery v. Weintraub, the landlord might have been "persuaded" by the factfinder's recommendations if the landlord believed that his failure to do so would produce a consumer boycott of his moorage facilities. If "moral suasion" is read this way, it would appear that there is a greater potential for effectiveness when at least one of the parties is a governmental entity.

At the same time, it should be noted that, notwithstanding the above observations about landlords' probable reactions, parties in the private and public sectors will often be persuaded by a factfinder's recommendations. Factfinders are mutually chosen by the disputing parties. They are selected because of the parties' confidence in their expertise, objectivity and fairness. Many people, if not most, want to do the "right thing"--whether in fixing rents, setting wages, resolving personal injury claims or consumer complaints. Although the factfinder's recommendations are ordinarily not legally binding upon the parties, they will each have had something like a "day in court." Unless they severely object to those recommendations, there is often strong reason to accept them. Whether one attributes this to "moral suasion" or to the parties' recognition of the "rightness" of the factfinder's recommendations, a dispute will have been resolved without ordinary judicial mechanisms having been invoked.

CHAPTER SIX
THE MINI-TRIAL

A. FIRST ANNUAL JUDICIAL CONFERENCE--FEDERAL CIRCUIT, REMARKS OF PROFESSOR ERIC GREEN AND HONORABLE JOE MORRIS (Page 127)

REMARKS OF PROFESSOR GREEN (Page 127)

The excerpt suggests that the mini-trial is a more effective dispute resolution device than direct negotiations between the parties' attorneys. If so, to what extent is this caused by the failure of attorneys to accurately communicate an opponent's position to their own clients--not as a result of wilfull concealment or misrepresentation, but simply because indirect communication is inevitably less accurate than direct communication? Could this weakness in normal negotiation procedures be cured by encouraging the presence of the affected clients during negotiations between attorneys?

Although attorneys generally negotiate with one another out of the presence of their respective clients, they do have ethical obligations to convey offers made by the other side to their clients, and not to refuse offers that the clients are willing to accept. Would special problems arise if the attorneys negotiated in the clients' presence? Is there a risk that a client, not being aware of the legal ramifications of the case, would reveal damaging facts that the attorney would prefer not to reveal, at least not during the negotiations? Or that, because of ill feelings between the parties, the client's participation would destroy the decorum of the negotiations? The mutual presence of opposing parties is a regular, if not indispensable, feature of mediation. In the just-described negotiation situation, however, the attorney serves as an advocate and not as a mediator. Why should that make a difference with respect to whether the presence of clients will help or hinder the negotiations?

REMARKS OF JUDGE MORRIS (Page 127)

One of the points stressed in this excerpt, as in Professor Green's, is the non-binding character of the mini-trial. Despite its non-binding character, however, mini-trials have in many cases induced parties to settle their disputes. This would suggest that factfinding also holds much promise as a dispute resolution mechanism.

Like a factfinder, the mini-trial's neutral advisor evaluates the facts and the strengths and weaknesses of each party's case. That evaluation, coupled with the opportunity each party has to hear the other party's "best case," are powerful inducements to settlement. The roles of the fact-finder and the mini-trial neutral advisor differ in other respects, however. For one thing, the neutral advisor merely predicts how a court might decide the case if it went to trial. The factfinder's recommendations, by contrast, are more than a prediction; they are a determination, concededly non-binding, of the rights and obligations of the parties. In addition, the mini-trial's neutral advisor is bound to keep the fact and the content of the proceedings confidential. Factfinding, however, contemplates the publication of the factfinder's recommendations in order to generate public pressure upon the parties to accept them.

<u>NOTES AND PROBLEMS FOR DISCUSSION</u> (Page 133)

<u>Note 1</u> (Page 133): Unless one assumes that in getting ready for ordinary litigation, attorneys waste much time, it is obvious that the more time that is spent preparing for the presentation of a case the more thorough will that preparation be. Yet one of the advertised virtues of the mini-trial is that it involves less preparation time for attorneys and parties than does an ordinary trial. However, the "dog and pony show," to use Professor Green's phrase, that the mini-trial represents, does provide the parties with much more information about the other side's case than they would ordinarily have. In participating in what might be described as a high stakes "moot court" exercise, the parties are likely to see a case in an entirely different light than when ordinary negotiations occur, even with the aid of prior discovery procedures.

<u>Note 2</u> (Page 133): Mini-trials will often not lead to a settlement. In those instances, they merely increase the parties' costs: Their attorneys must be paid for their presentations before the neutral advisor, and the neutral advisor must be paid for hearing the matter and for related expenses. While those costs are bearable if the disputants are wealthy corporations and the stakes are high, they may be unduly burdensome for persons of ordinary means. It is also possible that the more complex the issue or issues dividing the parties, the more effective will a mini-trial be. If the issues are relatively simple, the parties can gain an appreciation of the other side's position, and be able to evaluate the case without a mini-trial. This may explain why most of the literature dealing with the mini-trial has dealt with its use in inter-corporate dispute resolution.

<u>Note 3</u> (Page 133): The obvious incentive to present

the best case is to convince the opposing party to settle on favorable terms. However, trial strategy, unlike facts, is not subject to discovery. This could restrain a party's presentation in a mini-trial. It can be argued that the risks are greater here than in face-to-face negotiations, since a negotiator does not necessarily reveal trial strategy when discussing the case directly with opposing counsel. Non-binding factfinding and non-binding arbitration, on the other hand, would appear to present similar risks, if they do not resolve the dispute, of premature revelations of trial strategy and tactics.

Note 4 (Page 134): It can be argued that an action for breach of contract should lie under these circumstances. As noted earlier, parties outside the labor relations field do not have a legal duty to negotiate with one another to resolve their disputes. Under the NLRA, such a duty does exist, although the Act expressly recognizes that neither party is required to agree to a proposal or make a concession. The premise of the duty-to-bargain requirement, is that many labor disputes will be resolved if such bargaining occurs. That premise is supported by the record. In a non-labor relations case, one who has agreed to take part in a mini-trial can be deemed to have assumed, by contract, a duty to bargain. Although there is no guarantee that the mini-trial will lead to a settlement, the effort, in the light of labor negotiations experience, is worthwhile. What remedies would be available? One is an injunction requiring the defaulting party to participate in the mini-trial; this would be the analogue of an NLRB order requiring a party to "cease and desist" refusing to bargain (which order is enforceable by a federal court's issuance of what amounts, in effect, to an injunction). If the case goes to trial, and the party who wanted to proceed with the mini-trial prevails, that party has a tenable claim for the attorney's fees incurred in trial. Although under the "American Rule," attorney's fees are not ordinarily recoverable absent a statute allowing this, the prevailing party can argue that the attorney fees were incurred as a direct result of the other party's refusal to participate in the mini trial that might have produced a settlement and thereby obviated the need to incur additional attorney's fees.

CHAPTER SEVEN
THE OMBUDSMAN

A. INTRODUCTION (Page 135)

BECKMAN v. DUNN (Page 135)

According to the court, because of the contents of his communication and the presence of a "conditionally privileged occcasion," the defendant did not defame the plaintiff when he responded to the University Ombudsman's inquiry as he did. Suppose a student's complaint filed with a University Ombudsman contains damaging and untrue allegations about Smith, a faculty member who is the object of the complaint? In the course of his investigation, the Ombudsman asks other university personnel about Smith's activities and character. In the end, the Ombudsman determines that the complaint is unfounded, and so informs the student. Does Smith have a cause of action for defamation against the student? Against the ombudsman? Should the same privilege apply to the student's complaint as is applied to a judicial pleading? Does it make any difference if the decision to establish the ombudsman position was made unilaterally by the university president? By a vote of the faculty at a general meeting which Smith attended--or did not attend?

The dispute giving rise to a complaint will often result from a misunderstanding, an error, or communication difficulties. Can an ombudsman mediate the dispute as well as a mediator designated for that purpose? Despite the remarks of Professor Gellhorn, quoted in the introduction to this section of the Casebook, there is a serious danger that those who are the objects of complaints filed with an ombudsman will perceive the ombudsman's role as that of an advocate for the complainant rather than a mediator. That perception may well inhibit them from accepting the ombudsman's recommended resolution of a particular problem, in cases where they might accept the same recommendation from a person with only a mediatory role.

NOTES AND PROBLEMS FOR DISCUSSION (Page 142)

Note 5 (Page 145): Kenai Peninsula held that a school district had no duty to bargain over a teacher union's demand for, among other things, a teacher ombudsman.

Note 6 (Page 146): Unlike the "Action Line" ombudsmen, the other types mentioned in the question are either: 1) not self-appointed; or 2) do not handle complaints against persons and entities not connected to the appointing organization. If an "Action Line" ombudsmen tries to persuade a person or entity complained against to redress the complainant's grievance on the basis of fairness, good public relations, and the like, there should be no "unauthorized practice of law" problem. If "Action Line" were to cite legal doctrine, however, a potential problem would arise. Although certain public agencies, such as the National Labor Relations Board, permit non-lawyers to appear on behalf of others, the non-lawyers who do this are union business agents and company personnel managers representing their own organizations, or members of those organizations.

Note 7 (Page 146): Compared to negotiation, the ombudsman device has certain advantages. As suggested in this chapter, certain people--e.g., prison inmates, students--may be inhibited from trying to resolve grievances directly with prison officials or university administrators, because of the authority relationship between them. The ombudsman serves as a buffer in such circumstances. The suggestion has already been made that the mediatory role of an ombudsmen may not be as effective as that of a true mediator because of the perception by parties who are complained against that the ombudsman is the complainant's advocate. To the extent that an ombudsman is empowered to publicize his or her findings, the function is not unlike that of a factfinder. To the extent that the right to publish is denied, the ombudsman resembles that of a neutral advisor in a mini-trial, although one or both of the parties may not perceive the ombudsman's function in those terms.

CHAPTER EIGHT
SMALL CLAIMS COURTS

A. INTRODUCTION (Page 147)

CITY AND COUNTY OF SAN FRANCISCO v. SMALL CLAIMS DIVISION, MUNICIPAL COURT, NORTH JUDICIAL DISTRICT, COUNTY OF SAN MATEO (Page 147)

Had the California Supreme Court not previously affirmed the denial of class certification in the San Jose case, would the plaintiffs have been better off bringing their suit in an ordinary trial court? Among the disadvantages they incur by suing in small claims court are: 1) the loss of the right to be represented by an attorney in court; 2) loss of rights to discovery; and 3) loss of the protection afforded by formal rules of evidence. Moreover, if they lose in Small Claims Court, they are not entitled to a trial de novo, whereas defendants who lose may appeal to the superior court for such a trial.

Having been well advised by attorneys before the small claims trial on how to conduct themselves, the plaintiffs may not have been unduly prejudiced by the lack of counsel in the courtroom--especially since the defendant is also precluded from being represented by counsel there. The lack of discovery might also not have been too significant; the frequency of plane arrivals and departures, and their noise levels, could easily be established without prior discovery.

The case does represent an extraordinary use of the small claims court. It appears to have been utilized mainly to circumvent the limitations on class actions prescribed by the California Supreme Court in the San Jose case (although the defendant's failure to challenge the consolidation of these individual claims in small claims court may not foreclose future challenges to such a procedure). By invoking the small claims procedure, plaintiffs also minimized their expenses for attorneys and shortened the time for decision. On the other hand, the defendant's right to a trial de novo if the plaintiffs win in small claims court could remove many of these advantages. The time required to reach a decision will be prolonged, plaintiffs would need (or would be well advised to be represented by) counsel, and evidentiary rules would probably be applicable.

The reason for the tentativeness of the last conclusion stems from the decision of the California Court of Appeal in Maldonado v. Superior Court, 162 Cal. App.3d 1259, 209 Cal.

Rptr. 199 (1984). Before January 1, 1983, Rule 155 of the California Rules of Court provided: "When an action commenced in the municipal or justice court is tried on appeal in the superior court, such trial shall be conducted pursuant to law and rules in all respects as other trials in the superior court are required to be conducted, except that no written findings of fact or conclusions of law shall be required."

On January 1, 1983, the California Judicial Council amended Rule 155 to read: "Trial shall be conducted informally as provided in Code of Civil Procedure section 117 except that attorneys may participate. No tentative decision or statement of decision shall be required."

Section 117, subdivision (a), provides in pertinent part: "The hearing and disposition of small claims actions shall be informal, the object being to dispense justice promptly between the parties. The parties shall have the right to offer evidence by witnesses at the hearing or, with the permission of the court, at another time. The judge may consult witnesses informally and otherwise investigate the controversy. If the defendant fails to appear, the judge shall still require plaintiff to present evidence to prove his claim. The Judge shall give judgment * * * ."

In Maldonado, the California Court of Appeal held that, despite the revision of Rule 155 to require informality in de novo trials of cases appealed from small claims court, the defendant tenant had a statutory right to a jury trial in her appeal from an adverse judgment in a small claims unlawful detainer action. Conceding that its ruling "may prove burdensome for some claimants, the plaintiff's interest in an expeditious disposition cannot outweigh the defendant's right to trial by jury in a proceeding to evict her from her home." 162 Cal. App.3d at 1269, 209 Cal. Rptr. at 205. Whether Maldonado would require adherence to formal evidentiary rules is questionable, however, since the Court of Appeal relied on special statutory provisions guaranteeing a right to jury trial in unlawful detainer actions.

NOTES AND PROBLEMS FOR DISCUSSION (Page 156)

Note 1 (Page 156): Although California does not deny corporations the right to be plaintiffs in small claims court, it does provide, as noted in the principal case, that "the convenience of parties and witnesses who are individuals shall prevail, to the extent possible, over the convenience of any other parties or witnesses." This would appear to be limited to preferences in scheduling of hearings and in the order of presentation of proof.

Should parties be allowed to be represented by counsel in small claims court, as in New York? Or is the California model, which excludes attorneys from small claims court proceedings, preferable? Since it is permissible for only one party to be represented by counsel, does this not provide an additional advantage to the wealthy plaintiff or defendant over an opponent of limited means? Although corporations may not sue in small claims court under the N.Y. City Civ. Ct. Act, will they not enjoy an advantage over a plaintiff of limited means who either cannot afford an attorney or will have to spend more for an attorney than his or her claim is worth? Are small claims judges, who presumably are sensitive to the equities involved in small claims actions, likely to bend over backwards in evaluating the claims or defenses of an unrepresented party?

Note 2 (Page 156): Judge Evans and Mr. Bulman make the following recommendation: "One procedure cannot replace the other. As a practical matter, arbitration might not be able to handle an avalanche of small claims if small claims parts were abolished. Lawyer arbitrators also might find it difficult to process *pro se* actions in their private offices because of the problem of keeping order without court security personnel, and without the indicia of judicial or even quasi-judicial authority in the presence of sometimes antagonistic *pro se* litigants. If, instead, arbitration were abolished, small claims procedures would be ill-equipped to cope with the variety of cases processed by arbitration, and the presence of lawyers would give rise to a motion practice not suited to small claims parts.

"In summary, both procedures should be improved, strengthened, and expanded because both are needed. * * * "

CHAPTER NINE
JUDICIAL INDUCEMENTS TO SETTLEMENT

A. INTRODUCTION (Page 157)

MAREK v. CHESNY (Page 158)

The fundamental problem in this case arises from the fact that the present wording of Rule 68, with respect to whether the inclusion of attorney's fees are within "costs," is ambiguous. Analytically, each side has strong arguments in support of its position. Because, as examined in the Notes below and in Justice Brennan's dissenting opinion, large policy matters are affected by the decision in the case, the ultimate resolution will require a revision of the rule or new legislation.

NOTES AND PROBLEMS FOR DISCUSSION (Page 183)

Note 1 (Page 183): As in the principal case, recoverable attorney's fees often amount to more than the judgment for the basic violation of law. Since, under the Court's decision, the plaintiff's post-offer attorney's fees can not be recovered if the judgment is less favorable than the offer, this would work to discourage the filing of civil rights actions, among others.

Note 2 (Page 183): Suppose a defendant offers $50,000 to settle plaintiff's claim. Plaintiff sincerely believes that at least $65,000 will be recovered at trial. Plaintiff's attorney, who doubts that, knows that his or her post-offer legal services will be worth an additional $75,000, but has an agreement with the client to be paid only from a court-ordered attorney's fees award. Now that the post-offer attorney's fees may not be recovered by a winning plaintiff if the amount awarded at trial is less than the Rule 68 offer, there is an inevitable conflict between the client and the attorney as to whether the offer should be accepted. Compounding the conflict is the Court's determination that the Rule 68 offer does not have to separately designate an amount for the alleged civil rights violation and one for attorney's fees. Unless their agreement specifies that the attorney will receive a designated percentage of any settlement amount, this is another potential source of conflict between the plaintiff and his or her attorney.

Note 3 (Page 183): Defendants might be induced to make settlement offers that are much higher than what they sincerely believe are merited. They would fear that if the plaintiffs went to trial and recovered even a small amount, they, defendants, would be liable for post-offer attorney's fees, although not for post-offer "costs." Since attorney's fees are generally much higher than traditional "costs," defendants might believe that they had to make such an unmerited high offer, in order to avoid trial and the accumulation of plaintiff's attorney's fees.

Here too, however, a potential source of conflict between the plaintiff and his or her attorney would be created. In a sense this is the reverse of the situation dealt with in Note 2, above. Suppose that the $50,000 offer made by the defendant is acceptable to the plaintiff, but plaintiff's attorney believes that if the case goes to trial, there is a possibility of recovering more than that amount. If the Brennan view had prevailed, the attorney would know that, even if the amount recovered at trial is less than $50,000, he or she would be compensated for the post-offer legal services. The client, however, would be saddled with the other "costs," as well as with a money judgment that is lower than what the defendant had offered in settlement.

REVISION OF FRCP RULE 68, COMMITTEE NOTE (Page 183)

NOTES AND PROBLEMS FOR DISCUSSION (Page 187)

Note 1 (Page 187): An important change effected by the proposed revision is to make it applicable to a defendant who unreasonably refuses a plaintiff's offer of settlement. This would tend to "balance" the picture somewhat. More important is the standard of reasonableness in determining whether either a defendant or plaintiff should be saddled with costs, including attorney's fees, where the amount recovered is, respectively, greater than or less than the settlement offer. That would appear to be a great improvement over the Marek reading of the present Rule 68, which requires a loss of post-offer attorney's fees by the plaintiff without regard to the reasonableness of his or her rejection of the offer at the time it was made. The revised rule also goes far beyond the present rule in providing for "sanctions," which may result not only in the loss of post-offer attorney's fees incurred by a plaintiff or defendant, but a ruling that a prevailing plaintiff pay the post-offer attorney's fees incurred by a losing defendant, if the plaintiff's refusal to accept the settlement offer is determined to have been "unreasonable." In some of its applications, this provision might violate the Rules Enabling Act. It will be recalled that the majority in Marek relied on the fact that the Civil Rights Attorney's Fees Awards Act of 1976 referred to the awarding of attorney's fees as part of costs." As Justice Brennan points out in dissent, however, other federal statutes allowing an award of attorney's fees are worded differently. The proposed new Rule 68 could survive a Rules Enabling Act challenge, however, because the offeror's attorney's fees are only one of several factors to be taken into account in determining the amount of any sanction to be imposed upon the offeree who rejected the offer unreasonably.

The ADR movement's principal aim is the avoidance of litigation, if equally satisfactory, or superior, results can be achieved through alternative processes. In examining conciliation and mediation, we have seen that when all other things are equal, voluntary procedures are preferable to mandatory ones. In addition, one cannot decide in the abstract whether settlement is superior to litigation; the answer is likely to differ in different situations. In civil rights litigation, for example, as in Marek, would American society have been better served if the case had been settled before trial? Or does it gain more by having a judicial determination that the police officers had violated decedent's constitutional rights when they shot and killed him, and that the damages amounted to a particular sum?

CHAPTER TEN
SETTLEMENT

A. INTRODUCTION (Page 188)

B. CIVIL (Page 188)

1. INTERPRETING SETTLEMENT AGREEMENTS (Page 188)

PRESS MACHINERY CORPORATION v. SMITH R.P.M. CORPORATION (Page 192)

The case illustrates the principle that settlement agreements are just that, agreements, and thus subject to normal rules for interpreting contract language. Parties who draft such an agreement should take care that it accurately reflects their understanding about its scope, and particularly what future occurrences may be covered by it.

NOTES AND PROBLEMS FOR DISCUSSION (Page 192)

Note 1 (Page 192): Had the words, "or in any way pertaining to" been omitted from the release portion of the settlement agreement, Smith R.P.M's position would clearly have been strengthened. There are several possible explanations for why this was not done. One is that the attorneys simply overlooked the problems that the inclusion of this language might cause. Another is that the Court is correct in concluding that, when the settlement agreement was made, the parties' intended that PMC be permitted to complete its installation contract with the Kansas City Star, regardless of whether it used Smith R.P.M's unpatented or patented systems.

Note 2 (Page 192): Concerning duress, Sistrom v. Anderson states: "The test in any case is whether the complaining party was or was not in a position to exercise his own will. If the unlawful threats overcome the will of the person threatened, and 'induce him to do an act which he would not otherwise have done and which he was not bound to do,' duress, as it is viewed today, is effectuated. 5 Williston on Contract, § 1605." 124 P.2d at 376 (Emphasis supplied.) A fundamental inquiry, therefore, is whether a threat to sue is unlawful. In some states, as indicated in the following Note, certain threats to induce the payment of money actually owed constitute the crime of extortion. However, the California statute examined in that Note, refers to "a wrongful use of force or fear, or under color of official right." A creditor's mere assertion that, unless he or she is paid money owed by a debtor, suit will be brought, is not likely to fall within the scope of that language.

As for malicious prosecution, although some jurisdictions limit that cause of action to bad faith prosecution of criminal matters, Guth v. Walker, cited in the Note, others permit it when damages have been incurred "from a previous civil or criminal proceeding, which was commenced, or continued without probable cause, but with malice, and which has terminated unsuccessfully." Riegel (47 F. Supp. at 293). Even in such jurisdictions, however, where the affluent company has sued, it can hardly be claimed that the company did so without probable cause.

As illustrated by the principal case, the pleadings in a suit can shed much light on what parties intended when they concluded a settlement agreement. Although those intentions may be proved by utterances, writings and other evidence in the case of pre-suit settlement agreements, the pleadings can facilitate such proof.

Note 3 (Page 193): In Lindenbaum v. State Bar, an attorney made threats of action injurious to a client and his wife to force payment of the attorney's bill after the client had filed a bankruptcy petition. He also, with a punitive motive, wrote to the immigration authorities to incite an investigation of his client's wife as a supposed alien. Held: The attorney's action involved moral turpitude warranting a six-month suspension from law practice, although the money may have been justly due the attorney.

2. JURISDICTION TO ENFORCE SETTLEMENT AGREEMENTS (Page 194)

EQUAL EMPLOYMENT OPPORTUNITY COMMISSION v. HENRY BECK (Page 194)

Had the court ruled that there was no federal jurisdiction to entertain the EEOC's suit for specific enforcement of the settlement agreement, several other avenues would have been available. First, the charging party, as a party to the settlement agreement, could have sued for specific enforcement in either a state or federal court. The problem here is that, since this would have been necessited by a determination that suits to enforce PDS agreements are not "actions brought under" Title VII, attorney's fees would not be awardable to the charging party even if she prevailed in her specific performance suit. Another possibility would have been for the Commission to investigate the charge and make a reasonable cause determination. As noted by the district court in Cleveland State University, however, that course would render pre-determination settlement agreements meaningless.

The court's reference to the EEOC as a "mediator" when talking about its conciliation function is another example of the frequent interchangeability of these terms. The question of jurisdiction to enforce a settlement agreement can also arise under the NLRA, as noted by the court.

NOTES AND PROBLEMS FOR DISCUSSION (Page 199):

Note 2 (Page 201): Although the complaint in Pierce Packing did not "limit" itself to seeking specific enforcement of a PDS, the Commission did raise the issue on appeal in that case,. Arguably, therefore, the Ninth Circuit's decision conflicts with that of the Fourth Circuit in Henry Beck. As for reconciling the two quoted statements from Henry Beck, it is entirely plausible that a suit can be "brought" under Title VII, although it does "not involve litigation of the underlying unfair employment practice charge," since the settlement came into being only after the Title VII charge had been filed.

The possibility of jurisdiction being sustained on the basis of 28 U.S.C. Sections 1331 and 1332 is remote. The "arising under" language of those sections has been strictly construed. Although the EEOC's specific enforcement action is arguably "brought under" Title VII, that does not mean that it "arises under" Title VII or Section 1331 or 1332 of the Judicial Code. As for Section 1343, the analytical problem is the same as the one that is raised by the "brought under" language of Title VII's Section 706(f)(3). Does the equitable relief allowed by Title VII include specific enforcement of a PDS agreement. If the answer is yes, then the Beck result is correct, and there would be no need to invoke Section 1343.

Note 3 (Page 202): In Bechtel, infra, the court noted that "Bechtel argues that its alleged boycott activities were beyond the scope of the anti-trust laws. Bechtel contends this means it was beyond the power of the district court to enter the decree or contrary to the public interest for it do so." The Ninth Circuit concludes, however, that there is a distinction between an error in decision and the want of power to decide. "If Bechtel is correct in its assertion that the boycott is beyond the reach of the antitrust laws, it proves at most that the complaint failed to state a cause of action. Such a failure is not a jurisdictional defect.

In Firefighters Local Union No. 1784 v. Stotts, on the

other hand, the Supreme Court, quoting System Federation No. 91 v. Wright, 364 U.S. 642, 651, 81 S.Ct. 368, 373, 5 L.Ed.2d 349 (1961), noted: "'[T]he District Court's authority to adopt a consent decree comes only from the statute which the decree is intended to enforce,'not from the parties' consent to the decree." 104 S.Ct. at 2587, n. 9. It concluded, among other things, that a modification of a consent decree in a Title VII action could not stand if it violated the policy of that statute. It read Title VII's remedial provisions as not permitting preferential hiring of persons who were not identifiable victims of an employer's discriminatory employment practices. For that reason, among others (including Title VII's express protection of rights under bona fide seniority systems), it reversed a lower's court's modification of a consent decree settling an employment discrimination suit, which modification had enjoined the employer from laying off minority persons hired pursuant to the decree when layoffs were required by economic exigency. If _Stotts_ controls this situation, Acme Corporation's motion to vacate the consent decree for exceeding the court's jurisdiction should succeed; for, if _Henry Beck_'s holding that a pre-determination settlement agreement is "brought under" Title VII is correct, then _a fortiori_ an agreement to settle a Title VII suit is at least "brought under" and possibly "arises under" Title VII.

3. THE SETTLEMENT AGREEMENT AND THE PUBLIC INTEREST (Page 202)

UNITED STATES v. BECHTEL CORPORATION (Page 202)

Among other things, this case demonstrates that consent decrees, though judicial acts, are still contracts between the parties who agreed to their entry. The traditional grounds for relief from a contractual obligation therefore apply to such decrees: a party's repudiation of the agreement, its failure to comply with one or more of its conditions, the absence of valid consent to the agreement, or a violation of public policy (read "public interest") in the terms of the agreement. The case also illustrates that settlement agreements, whether incorporated in a consent decree or not, can have important effects on persons other than those who conclude them. Under the APPA, the _Bechtel_ court concludes: "The court's role in protecting the public interest is one of insuring that the government has not breached its duty to the public in consenting to the decree. The court is required to determine not whether a particular decree is the one that will best serve society, but whether the settlement is 'within the reaches of the public interest.'"

NOTES AND PROBLEMS FOR DISCUSSION (Page 210)

Note 1 (Page 210): Consent decrees, unlike private unrecorded settlements between the parties, are: 1) matters of public record; 2) of possible precedential value in future cases; 3) thereby establishing public norms governing the behavior of others. At the same time, because the parties are given much latitude in devising the terms of the decree, they may differ drastically from what a court would have ordered had the case gone to trial. The APPA obviously minimizes the latter possibility in that the court must be sensitive to the public interest in deciding whether to confirm the consent decree. However, the relaxed attitude of the courts toward their duties respecting the public interest, as indicated by the discussion in Bechtel and emphasized above, suggests that the public interest may, in a practical sense, often be slighted when a court approves a consent decree.

Note 2 (Page 210): In Spomer, the court noted that an agreement of the parties concerning visitation does not bind a trial court when the best interest of the child are to the contrary. In Miller, a post-nuptial agreement provided that custody of a minor child was to be given to the father. The trial court found this arrangement invalid. Although the Pennsylvania Superior Court reversed the trial court for having applied the discredited "tender years doctrine," the Superior Court did not question the authority of the trial court to review the merits of the custody arrangement, in the light of the child's best interests.

4. THE SETTLEMENT AGREEMENT AND ADMINISTRATIVE DISCRETION (Page 210)

CITIZENS FOR A BETTER ENVIRONMENT v. GORSUCH (Page 210)

Among other things, this case illustrates advantages and drawbacks to administrative rule-making by negotiation. The issues dividing the majority and dissent can be profitably explored. Does the consent decree interfere with administrative discretion in violation of the separation of powers doctrine? Or does the EPA's consent distinguish this case from others in which courts have been reversed for interfering with administrative discretion? Is the line between "merits" and "procedures" as bright as the majority suggests? Or is the dissent correct in its suggestion that binding the agency to certain procedures will ultimately affect its substantive policies? Will the majority's analysis in this case always help persons or organizations who seek to protect the environment, or can it, as the dissent suggests, harm their interests? In that connection, would a consent decree incorporating "procedural" standards harmful to the interests of pro-environment groups and individuals be "consistent with the policy" of the Act? Isn't such consistency vital to the majority's position? Does it not distinguish the situation in this case from the one in Firefighters v. Stotts, discussed in this Manual at Note 3 following the discussion of Henry Beck, supra? In Stotts, the Supreme Court held that a modification of a consent decree in a Title VII action could not stand if it violated the policy of that statute. Here, however, the D.C. Circuit stresses that the consent decree is consistent with that policy.

NOTES AND PROBLEMS FOR DISCUSSION (Page 231)

Note 1 (Page 231): The inclusion of those provisions in the decree meant that the EPA was subject to a contempt action for failure to abide by its terms. This is a decided advantage for the environmental groups who, if they were limited to suing on the agreement alone, would first have to get a decree of specific performance before any contempt remedy would be feasible. If those provisions had been included in the agreement only, the separation-of-powers issue would also arguably not be implicated, at least insofar as the agreement standing alone is concerned. However, if the environmental groups sought specific performance of the agreement, or if the companies sought a judicial declaration of its invalidity or an injunction to prevent the agency from carrying out its terms, the court would still have to decide whether the requirements of the Administrative Procedure Act were observed. Since the APA does not require agencies to observe the same formalities when they promulgate rules governing their internal procedures as when they engage in substantive rule making, the companies would probably lose in such a suit as well--although the question of where to draw the line between procedures and substantive rules would still have to be answered. In such a case, it could also be argued that if a court enjoined an agency from carrying out the terms of its agreement, it would be interfering with the administrative discretion exercised by the agency when it concluded the agreement.

Note 2 (Page 231): First, it should be noted that the rule-making that occurred in this case resulted from the invocation of the adversarial judicial process. Second, the statement quoted from the principal case which extols the virtues of a less adversarial approach to developing regulations does not distinguish between procedural and substantive rules. Most important, however, are the concerns raised by dissent, and the ideas of Justice Douglas in the quoted excerpt in this Note. If we focus on an agency's substantive rules rather than those governing its internal procedures, are not fundamental questions of participation in the democratic process implicated? On the other hand, aren't many rules governing the behavior of persons in American society developed by courts when they decide cases between private individuals, or between individuals and government agencies?

5. CLASS ACTION SETTLEMENT AGREEMENTS (Page 232)

PARKER v. ANDERSON (Page 232)

Why does the court, in footnote 6, approve of the Second Circuit's language that "In fact there is no reason, at least in theory, why a satisfactory settlement could not amount to a hundredth or even a thousandth part of a single percent of the potential recovery?" The answer lies in the use of the word "potential." If the plaintiffs' chances of winning that amount at trial are doubtful, and, *a fortiori*, if there is a reasonable probability that plaintiffs will lose at trial, the court can approve a settlement amount that represents such a small portion of the "potential" recovery.

Why does the usual rule that "an attorney cannot settle his individual client's case without the authorization of the client" not apply in class actions? The answer: Although the attorney has been retained by the named parties, once a class has been certified the attorney's obligation runs to the class as a whole. In a sense, the class, including the absent members who, by definition, vastly outnumber the named members, becomes the attorney's client, rather than the individuals who retained the attorney in the first place.

NOTES AND PROBLEMS FOR DISCUSSION (Page 242)

Note 1 (Page 242): The statement by courts that in examining a proposed compromise in a class action suit, they "do not try the case" is valid only if one interprets this to mean that they do not subject the case to a full blown trial. On the other hand, in assessing the "factual and legal obstacles [to] prevailing on the merits," courts inevitably make tentative determinations about the merits of the case. This might be thought of as a form of "shallow trial," but a trial nevertheless.

Note 2 (Page 242): The court states: "The evil feared in some settlements--unscrupulous attorneys negotiating large attorney's fees at the expense of an inadequate settlement for the client--can best be met by a careful district judge, sensitive to the problem, properly evaluating the adequacy of the settlement for the class and determining and setting a reasonable attorney's fee in light of the Johnson standards." This would suggest that an attorney's fee that consumed 100% of the settlement fund would be an abuse of discretion. At the same time, the standards set forth here are extremely vague. By their very nature, class action settlements are likely to involve large sums that have to be divided among many individual class members. A pro-class presumption under those circumstances might be warranted. This is in contrast to attorney's fees that are authorized by statute or otherwise, which will often be awarded in suits in which an attorney represents an individual client. In such cases, it is not unusual for the attorney's fee award greatly to exceed the amount recovered by the individual plaintiff.

Note 3 (Page 243): In W.R. Grace and Company v. Local Union 759, which will be considered shortly and is reported at page 258 of the Casebook, the United States Supreme Court had to decide whether certain third parties are affected by a settlement agreement between others. By contrast, in Parker v. Anderson, as well as in the case before last, United States v. Bechtel Corporation, that third parties are affected by such settlement agreements had already been established--by Congress in Bechtel and in earlier court interpretations of FRCP Rule 23 in Parker.

Thus, in Bechtel, the APPA required a district court to determine that a consent judgment was in the public interest before it could be entered. Among other matters, in making this determination, the court could consider "the impact of entry of such judgment upon the public generally and individuals alleging specific injury from the violations set forth in the complaint including considerations of the public benefit, if any, to be derived from a determination of the issues at trial." APPA, 15 U.S.C. § 16(e)(2). As noted earlier, the Bechtel court concluded that its function was not "to determine * * * whether a particular decree is the one that will best serve society, but whether the settlement is 'within the reaches of the public interest.'"

In Parker the court states: "Rule 23(e) requires court approval of compromise settlements of class actions, but it is silent as to the standard to be applied. Nonetheless, the rubric is now well established that the court will not approve a settlement unless it is found to be fair, adequate, and reasonable."

The problems in both types of cases are, therefore, similar in that they require consideration of the interests of third parties who will be affected by the entry of the consent decree or approval of the settlement agreement. The devices resemble one another also in the degree and quality of consideration afforded to third party interests. However, they differ with respect to the sizes of the third-party groups, the entire public being the subject of inquiry under the APPA and only the class members (named as well as absent) in class action settlements. They differ also in the quality of scrutiny each is subjected to, and the attorney's fee problem which is more likely to be present in the class action settlement than in the consent decree.

6. SETTLEMENTS AND CLAIM PRECLUSION (Page 243)

ADAMS v. PROCTOR & GAMBLE MANUFACTURING CO. (Page 243)

NOTES AND PROBLEMS FOR DISCUSSION (Page 247)

Note 1 (Page 247): The principal difference between the majority and dissent in *Adams* is that of a literal interpretation of Section 706(f)(1) as opposed to an interpretation that considers ultimate congressional purposes and other provisions of Title VII. The major difficulty created for charging parties by the majority's holding is that, to avoid being bound by the settlement reached by the EEOC in its suit against the respondent, they would have to intervene in that suit. Although they might ultimately recover an attorney's fees award if they prevailed in that action, that award might be negligible if the court determined that their participation in the suit did not produce a higher judgment than the EEOC would have obtained in settlement or in trial. As a result, they might have difficulty retaining an attorney to represent them--or many attorneys might request "up front" payment for their services, which most charging parties could not satisfy.

In *General Telephone*, the Supreme Court enumerated ways that an employer sued in a class action by the EEOC can protect itself against subsequent suits by absent class members who had not filed charges with that agency. A strong argument can be made that, slightly modified, similar protections are available to an employer who settles with the EEOC, rather than allowing the case to be tried. For example, the employer can condition settlement on first learning how many, and which, charging parties would not wish to be bound by the settlement. In that way, the employer could assess the extent of its continued exposure after settlement.

Note 2 (Page 248): The problems confronting a charging party who intervenes in the EEOC's action are discussed in the preceding Note.

EQUAL EMPLOYMENT OPPORTUNITY COMMISSION v. CONSOLIDATED EDISON COMPANY OF NEW YORK, INC. (Page 248)

The ADEA and Title VII have similar aims: eliminating certain types of employment discrimination and making whole those who have been injured by such discrimination. The two Acts' different treatment of a charging party's right to interevene is, therefore, anomalous. It is not too surprising, however, given other procedural and substantive differences between the two statutes. As noted by the court, allowing aggrieved persons as well as the EEOC to sue for ADEA violations creates the problem of duplicative litigation. Congress resolved this by providing that commencement of the EEOC suit terminates the right of "any person to bring" such action. Intervention is also denied presumably to give the EEOC complete control over the conduct of the suit, including any settlement that may be reached in connection with it. As a policy matter this is fraught with difficulties, as the court itself acknowledges. In earlier cases, we have explored potential conflicts of interest between attorneys and clients in the process of settlement. The EEOC is charged with eliminating the discriminatory employment practice for the protection of the general public; but it is also charged with assuring that victims of that discrimination are made whole. It will often be difficult to achieve both goals simultaneously; and there is no guarantee that the EEOC, in effecting a settlement, will not be motivated by its obligations to the general public more than by those it owes to the actual victims of discrimination.

NOTES AND PROBLEMS FOR DISCUSSION (Page 256)

Note 1 (Page 256): Given the literal language of Section 7(c)(1), the Burns result seems eminently correct. In the light of Consolidated Edison's discussion of congressional intent in enacting that section, however, Castle v. Sangamo would appear to be more consistent with that intent. If Congress wanted to place primary responsibility in the hands of the EEOC for litigating ADEA claims, then it should not make much difference whether the charging party had filed suit before or after the EEOC. Still, there is that literal language * * *.

Note 2 (Page 256): One can only speculate as to this. Certainly, the "sweet" includes the right to legal redress for age-based employment discrimination, a right that did not, and as a general rule still does not, exist at common law. In addition, the right to be represented free of charge by the EEOC is a valuable one that might also be considered part of the "sweet."

Note 3 (Page 256): This question is examined in the discussion of *Consolidated Edison*, supra. It is difficult, to say the least, to discover any policy justification for the differences between a charging party's right to intervene in an EEOC age discrimination suit under the ADEA and an EEOC suit alleging race, national origin, religion, or sex discrimination.

Note 4 (Page 257): There does not appear to be any more rationality in the differences in the treatment accorded to intervention by the NLRA and the ADEA.

7. SETTLEMENTS AND OBLIGATIONS TO THIRD PARTIES (Page 258)

W.R. GRACE AND COMPANY v. LOCAL UNION 759, INTERNATIONAL UNION OF THE UNITED RUBBER, CORK, LINOLEUM AND PLASTIC WORKERS OF AMERICA (Page 258)

Although dealing primarily with the preclusive (or non-preclusive) effects of a settlement agreement, the case also raises several arbitration issues. Most will be dealt with in the following chapter on arbitration. For present purposes, it is sufficient to note: 1) the policy of judicial deference to arbitration awards on the theory that the parties have chosen an arbitrator, rather than a court, to decide disputes arising under their collective bargaining agreement; 2) the general rule that prior arbitral awards are not binding upon subsequent arbitrators hearing similar disputes between the same parties.

Although this is a labor case, the problem it raises can arise in other contexts. The basic principle it exemplifies is that if A has an obligation to B, A can not be absolved of that obligation by its settlemement of a separate dispute with C, in which settlement B has not participated. Moreover, that a trial court has erroneously ruled that A's agreement with C does have this effect will not protect A if A takes action in reliance upon that ruling, if the ruling is ultimately reversed by a higher court.

Anyone contemplating settling a dispute with another person or entity should, therefore, take into account obligations he or she has toward third persons that will be rendered difficult, or impossible, to perform as a result of the settlement agreement. Although the third parties can sometimes be induced to participate in joint settlement negotiations, thereby avoiding the W. R. Grace type of problem if they approve of the settlement agreement, this is not likely to occur very often.

NOTES AND PROBLEMS FOR DISCUSSION (Page 267)

Note 1 (Page 267): By noting that "Barrett's award neither mandated layoffs nor required that layoffs be conducted according to the collective bargaining agreement," the Court strongly intimates that the inclusion of either of these orders in the award would have conflicted with the district court's order, if the latter were properly characterizable as an injunction. Because the Court also suggests that the district court order was merely a declaratory judgment, however, including such provisions in the arbitral award would be arguably valid.

Note 2 (Page 267): The EEOC's conciliation and settlement practices should be examined in responding to this question. One should distinguish pre-determination settlement agreements (PDS) from settlement agreements concluded after the EEOC has found reasonable cause to believe that a respondent employer, labor organization or employment agency has committed an unlawful employment practice. In the PDS situation, the EEOC essentially allows the charging party or parties and the respondent to work out whatever agreement they wish, although the EEOC is a signatory to such agreements. (The EEOC's signing the agreement gives it the standing to sue to enforce it in cases like Henry Beck, supra.) In post-determination conciliation agreements, the EEOC's role is different, however. In such cases, it has already conducted an investigation and made a reasonable cause determination. (Note that the EEOC's reasonable cause determination is neither res judicata nor admissible in any subsequent court trial of the employment discrimination claim). It has also decided what an appropriate remedy for such a violation would be. Its role in conciliation includes that of persuading not only the respondent but also the charging party to resolve the dispute along the lines the EEOC thinks appropriate. The ultimate decision is up to the parties, but if a charging party refuses to settle along the terms suggested by the EEOC, the EEOC cannot settle on the latter's behalf. What it can and does do to pressure the charging party is to say that if those terms are not accepted, the EEOC will dismiss the case, and transmit a right-to-sue letter to the charging party. This means that the charging party can bring his or her own suit, but that the EEOC will not sue on behalf of the charging party, even though it has found reasonable cause to believe that the respondent committed an unlawful employment practice and might otherwise have sued if the respondent alone had rejected the settlement terms deemed appropriate by the EEOC.

These practices indicate that the EEOC cannot bind a non-approving charging party or parties to a settlement agreement.

B. CRIMINAL (Page 267)

1. PLEA BARGAINING AS VIEWED BY "CIVIL LIBERTARIANS" (Page 267)

SANTOBELLO v. NEW YORK (Page 267)

Santobello had actually entered a guilty plea in reliance upon the prosecutor's promise not to make any sentencing recommendation. Compare the next case, Mabry v. Johnson, in which the prosecutor changed his mind about the plea bargain before the defendant had relied upon it.

NOTES AND PROBLEMS FOR DISCUSSION (Page 274)

Note 1 (Page 274): Both Press Machinery Corporation v. Smith R.P.M. Corporation and *Henry Beck* involved alleged breaches of settlement agreements, which is at stake in *Santobello* as well. In *Press Machinery*, PMC sought and obtained declaratory relief only. By contrast, in *Henry Beck* the EEOC sought and obtained specific performance of the settlement agreement's terms. However, in *Santobello* the petitioner sought to rescind the plea bargain and to stand trial on the charges. A majority of the Court holds that the prosecution's breach of the plea bargain, although inadvertent, entitles the petitioner to relief. It leaves to the state court, however, the decision as to the form of that relief: whether it should be withdrawal of the guilty plea, as requested by the petitioner, or specific performance of the plea bargain, with resentencing by a different judge.

Justice Douglas' concurring opinion is especially instructive in setting forth the reasons for civil libertarians' apprehensions about plea bargaining. These boil down to a concern that the state wins a guilt determination without having satisfied the burdens that it would have to meet if the case were tried: jury trial, strong presumption of innocence, strict evidence rules, etc.

There is no reason to believe that the criticisms by Professor Fiss and others are based on anything other than an effort to protect the integrity of the criminal adjudicative process and, more fundamentally, the rights of all persons accused of crime (many of whom will be innocent) to the traditional safeguards against erroneous verdicts.

Note 2 (Page 275): The comments in the preceding Note apply also to Professor Schulhofer's statement. Professor Schulhofer's article raises another question, however--namely, is it feasible to have bench trials (i.e., without a jury) in all cases that are currently settled by plea bargaining? The traditional wisdom, as suggested in Santobello, is that the criminal justice system would collapse if jury trials were held in all such cases. Although bench trials are much less complex than jury trials, it is doubtful that the criminal justice system would escape injury if this recommendation were adopted. It should be noted, however, that persons accused of crime would often prefer to enter a bargained plea than to stand trial before even a judge alone. The state's savings of time, money, energy and other resources in accepting such plea bargains would still be strong reasons for continuing the practice.

Note 3 (Page 275): In Santobello, it is clear that the defendant seeks to withdraw the guilty plea because his new attorney has discerned weaknesses in the prosecution's case that could lead to a verdict of acquittal, or even a pretrial dismissal of the charges. Should not the petitioner be bound by his first attorney's appraisal of the case? Or was that appraisal so deficient that it constituted ineffective assistance of counsel that could lead to a subsequent release on habeas corpus? As for specific performance, a defendant would choose this route if he and/or his attorney believed that he would be convicted in a trial. Although, as in Santobello, a judge might decide to impose a harsh sentence on a convicted defendant without regard to a prosecutor's recommendation, the defendant's chances for a lighter sentence are greater if the prosecutor is required to abide by his or her promise not to recommend a particular sentence. The new appraisal of the defendant's case by his second attorney might be a sufficient circumstance to warrant granting his request to withdraw his earlier guilty plea, rather than requiring specific performance of the original plea bargain.

MABRY v. JOHNSON (Page 275)

The essence of this case resides in the habeas corpus

relief sought by the defendant, which is available only when a person is "in custody in violation of the Constitution or laws or treaties of the United States." A unanimous Court tells us that the mere breach of promise by the prosecutor is insufficient to justify such relief, since the defendant did not, as in Santobello, rely on that promise when he pleaded guilty. As the notes following the case indicate, this result is different from what occurs when there is a breach of a settlement agreement in a civil proceeding, where the mutual promises are sufficient in and of themselves to form a binding contract. Once again, however, the difference in treatment stems from the defendant's invocation of the habeas corpus remedy.

NOTES AND PROBLEMS FOR DISCUSSION (Page 279)

Note 1 (Page 279): Many of the questions posed in this Note are answered in the above discussion of the case. In Carey v. Piphus, a student had been suspended from a public elementary school, and another from a public secondary school, without being given an adjudicatory hearing. In an action brought under 42 U.S.C. § 1983, the United States Supreme Court held that, absent proof of actual injury, the students were entitled to receive only nominal damages ($1.00). Because, as noted in Mabry, state law did not require the trial court to accept a prosecutor's sentencing recommendation, it would be difficult, if not impossible, for the defendant to prove actual injury under the facts of that case. Even if that hurdle could be overcome, Imbler v. Pachtman would present an insurmountable obstacle to a civil damage recovery. In Imbler, petitioner was released on habeas corpus because of his proof that the prosecutor had knowingly used false testimony and suppressed material evidence at his trial. In reviewing the subsequent Section 1983 suit, however, the Supreme Court held that a state prosecuting attorney who acts within the scope of his duties in initiating and pursuing a criminal prosecution and in presenting the State's case is absolutely immune from a civil suit for damages under § 1983 for alleged deprivations of the accused's constitutional rights.

Note 2 (Page 280): Footnote 11 merely points out that one of the options available to the court was to permit the defendant to replead. Unlike Justice Marshall's concurring opinion in Santobello, however, it did not suggest that this was the preferred course of action.

Note 3 (Page 280): Reversing the Ninth Circuit, the Supreme Court in Benchimol held per curiam that the government had not breached the plea bargain under the circumstances described in this Note. Among other things, the Court stated:

"It may well be that the Government in a particular case might commit itself to 'enthusiastically' make a particular recommendation to the Court, and it may be that the Government in a particular case might agree to explain to the Court the reasons for the Government's making a particular recommendation. But respondent does not contend, nor did the Court of Appeals find that the Government had in fact undertaken to do either of these things here.

* * *

" * * * The Government suggests that spreading on the record its reasons for agreement to a plea bargain in a particular case--for example, that it did not wish to devote scarce resources to a trial of this particular defendant, or that it wished to avoid calling the victim as a witness--would frequently harm, rather than help, the defendant's quest for leniency. These may well be reasons why the defendant would not wish to exact such a committment from the Government, but for purposes of this case it is enough that no such agreement was made in fact. Since Rule 11(e) speaks generally of the plea bargains that the parties make, it was error for the Court of Appeals to imply as a matter of law a term which the parties themselves did not agree upon." ___ U.S. at ___, 105 S.Ct. at 2105, ___ L.Ed.2d at ___.

<u>BORDENKIRCHER</u> <u>v.</u> <u>HAYES</u> (Page 280)

This case raises a variant of the "power versus reason in negotiations" question examined earlier. The majority acknowledges that the prosecutor, by threatening to seek an indictment of the defendant under the Kentucky Habitual Criminal Act if he did not accept a five-year sentence for uttering a forged instrument, was merely using "leverage" to reach a plea bargain (read "settlement agreement"). However, the prosecutor's power to do this is limited by constitutional constraints. Although the majority approves of the prosecutor's actions here, it stresses that he apprised the defendant of his intention to seek the Habitual Criminal Act indictment during the negotiations. Implicit in that emphasis is the suggestion that, had he not done that, and had he sought the new indictment after the defendant rejected the proferred plea bargain, prosecutorial vindictiveness would have been established.

Had the prosecutor offered adverse or lenient treatment for some person other than the accused, the majority notes, this "might pose a greater danger of inducing a false guilty plea by skewing the assessment of the risks a defendant must consider." Such conduct could, therefore, be found to violate the defendant's constitutional rights. Recall the problem examined in Note 3 following Press Machinery Corporation at page 193 of the Casebook.

If the defendant in Bordenkircher had prevailed in the Supreme Court he would have clearly won a personal victory. Would his triumph have also represented a victory for other persons accused of crime? All the Justices acknowledge that a prosecutor's decision to "overcharge" is in a practical sense unreviewable. Yet none would object to a prosecutor reducing a more serious charge in return for a defendant's pleading guilty to a lesser charge. Are the "reasons of fairness why the charges should be presented at the beginning of the bargaining process, rather than as a filliped threat at the end," suggested in footnote 2 of Justice Blackmun's dissenting opinion, persuasive? Would this practice be likely to produce more, or less, severe sentences?

NOTES AND PROBLEMS FOR DISCUSSION (Page 290)

Note 2 (Page 290): Part of the answer to this question appears in the discussion of the case, supra. In both civil and criminal contexts, the process of negotiation, with each side uncertain of the consequences of not reaching a settlement, is involved. That uncertainty gives each side a degree of "power" or "leverage" in the negotiations. However, the effect of the Constitution in the distribution of that power differs markedly in the criminal and civil areas. The constitutional safeguards of the Bill of Rights, generally applicable to the states via the Fourteenth Amendment's due process clause, create many possibilities for an acquittal or of a reversal of a conviction. They thus enhance the accused's bargaining power. At the same time, Bordenkircher makes clear that prosecutors violate the due process rights of defendants if, without informing the latter of their intention to do so, they vindictively file more serious charges against them because they have rejected a proferred plea bargain. This represents a weakening of the prosecutor's power which might be redressed by "overcharging," a process that is not without its dangers to the prosecutor).

4. "PLEA BARGAINING" AS VIEWED BY "LAW-AND-ORDER" PROPONENTS (Page 290)

PEOPLE v. SUPERIOR COURT COUNTY OF LOS ANGELES (Page 290)

NOTES AND PROBLEMS FOR DISCUSSION (Page 302)

Note 1 (Page 302): The important distinction between an "indicated sentence" and a "plea bargain" is that the "indicated sentence" is not conditioned upon the defendant pleading guilty. The court simply announces what sentence it intends to impose if defendant is convicted regardless of whether that conviction is based on a guilty plea or a trial. When the court has announced an "indicated sentence," it would appear that defendants have nothing to lose if they stand trial and force the prosecution to prove their guilt; even if they are convicted, their sentence will be the same as the one they would have received if they had entered a guilty plea. Many defendants who are convinced of their guilt will nevertheless plead guilty on the basis of the court's indicated sentence, simply to avoid the trauma and expense of a trial whose outcome seems foreordained.

If the court indicates a sentence, the defendant's plea need not be conditional to, in effect, circumvent the apparent intention of Proposition 8's sponsors. If the court breaches its promise with regard to the indicated sentence, the defendant could undoubtedly withdraw his or her plea because of detrimental reliance on that promise.

The literal language of the first sentence of Section 1192.7(a) would appear to permit the conclusion of a plea bargain prior to the filing of an indictment or an information. This could be done even after a preliminary hearing has been commenced, since a preliminary hearing precedes the filing of an information. As for plea bargains without the acquiescence of the prosecuting attorney, the principal case makes clear that this would represent a usurpation by the judiciary of powers reserved to prosecutorial authorities.

Note 2 (Page 302): As indicated earlier, plea bargaining is far from an unmixed blessing for persons accused of crime. There is always the danger that a person who is totally innocent of any crime will be induced to plead guilty to a criminal charge out of fear that he or she will be erroneously found guilty of a more serious crime if the latter is charged and tried. This danger is mitigated somewhat by the right to counsel in such negotiations, but it is a danger nevertheless. Above all, society as a whole may suffer if prosecutors procure convictions "on the cheap," i.e., without having to prove to a judge or jury, beyond a reasonable doubt, in a proceeding that recognizes constitutional evidentiary privileges and other prophylatic rules, that the defendant has in fact committed the crime of which he or she is accused.

Moreover, in addition to the advantages for the prosecution cited in the ballot argument opposing Proposition 8, there can be little doubt that the entire system of criminal prosecution would suffer greatly if the overwhelming majority of criminal cases were not settled by plea bargains.

CHAPTER ELEVEN
ARBITRATION

A. INTRODUCTION (Page 304)

B. THE PAST ATTITUDE OF THE COURTS TOWARDS ARBITRATION (Page 307)

KULUKUNDIS SHIPPING CO., S/A v. AMTORG TRADING CORPORATION (Page 307)

This case is included primarily for its textual description of the evolving status of arbitration in English and American law. Although the answer is obvious to most students, it may still be worthwhile to ask the class to define an "executory agreement to arbitrate" (definition: one that has not yet been performed; more precisely, one in which an arbitration award has not yet been rendered). The analytical and policy questions raised in *Kulukundis* are examined in the Notes and Problems for Discussion that follow it.

NOTES AND PROBLEMS FOR DISCUSSION (Page 315)

Note 4 (Page 318): In Gaslin, Inc. v. L.G.C. Exports, Inc., a franchise agreement, which was executed one year before the state adopted the Uniform Arbitration Act, provided for arbitration of disputes "in accordance with the least expensive procedure of the American Arbitration Association." *Held*: Although the dispute arose after the state adopted the Uniform Arbitration Act, it was governed by common law principles rather than by statute. "Accordingly," the trial court committed an error of law in determining that [the appellant] had waived his right to challenge the arbitrator's award by failing to follow the procedures set forth in the * * * Act."

C. STATE VERSUS FEDERAL LAW (Page 319)

BERNHARDT v. POLYGRAPHIC CO. OF AMERICA, INC. (Page 319)

Many of the cases in the Casebook arise under state arbitration statutes. However, the Federal Arbitration Act (formerly United States Arbitration Act) is central to the examination of the American law of arbitration. To avoid possible constitutional problems, the Court in *Bernhardt* interprets § 3 of the FAA, which provides for a stay of actions in the federal courts of issues referable to arbitratration, as applying only to the two types of contracts (maritime and those involving commerce) whose arbitration clauses are made "valid, irrevocable, and enforceable" by § 2 of the Act. Because the case is in federal court on the basis of diversity of citizenship, however, the Court examines whether granting the requested stay to permit arbitration would, for purposes of Erie and Guaranty Trust, be permissible as a procedural mechanism or prohibited as a substantive rule, in the sense that it is "outcome determinative." Interestingly, in deciding that requiring arbitration here would be "outcome determinative," the Court reiterates many of the characterizations of the arbitration process that persuaded Judge Story in Tobey that executory agreements to arbitrate should not be specifically enforceable.

NOTES AND PROBLEMS FOR DISCUSSION (Page 326)

Note 1 (Page 326): It can be argued that the more expansive interpretation of the meaning of "commerce" that the Court has offered in recent years could lead to a different result in a Bernhardt-type case were one to arise today. However, it would still be incumbent upon the party seeking to invoke the FAA to "make a showing" that he or she was "working 'in commerce, was producing goods for commerce, or was engaging in activity that affected commerce, within the meaning of our decisions." (Emphasis supplied). Perhaps the plaintiff in Bernhardt could have prevailed on the arbitration issue had he made such a showing. However, because of the court's restrictive interpretation of "commerce" at that time, it might have been difficult, if not impossible, for him to do so.

In Burke County Public Schools Board of Education v. Shaver Partnership, the North Carolina Supreme Court, characterized the position of the majority in Prima Paint v. Flood & Conklin, 388 U.S. 395, 87 S.Ct.1801, 18 L.Ed.2d 1270 (1967) as follows:

" * * * Congress intended the federal act to encompass not only contracts for the interstate shipment of goods but also contracts merely 'relating to interstate commerce.' Furthermore the majority did not view 'relating to interstate commerce' as equivalent to 'relating to the actual physical interstate shipment of goods.' Instead, it viewed the phrase 'relating to interstate commerce' in a broader, more encompassing sense. * * * Had the Court's majority, while holding that the act was not restricted to contracts for the interstate shipment of goods, intended to restrict the act's applicability to contracts involving or relating to the interstate shipment of goods we think it would have said so, especially since such a restriction would have conflicted both with language from an earlier opinion, [Bernhardt] and with earlier lower court decisions." 279 S.E.2d at 820.

The Burke County court concluded, therefore, that "a personal service contract which contemplates substantial interestate activity is a contract evidencing a transaction involving commerce within the meaning of the act." 279 S.E.2d at 822 (emphasis supplied).

SOUTHLAND CORPORATION v. KEATING (Page 327)

Although both decisions are rather long, it is desirable, though not indispensable, to have the class read this case and the next one, Lincoln Mills, before starting the discussion of Keating. There is an interaction between the two cases which can be overlooked if they are read in separate sessions.

NOTES AND PROBLEMS FOR DISCUSSION (Page 348)

Note 1 (Page 348): At first blush, there appears to be a glaring internal contradiction in the majority's conclusion in footnote 10 that, although the FAA "creates federal substantive law requiring parties to honor arbitration agreements, it does not create any independent federal-question jurisdiction." This principle also apppears to be at odds with the Court's holding in City of Milwaukee, which read Lincoln Mills as a case "arising under" federal common law, thus satisfying the requirements of Article III of the federal constitution. However, the negative implications of the words of §§ 3 and 4, also quoted in footnote 10 of the majority opinion in Keating, seem to support its conclusion on the federal jurisdiction question.

Note 2 (Page 348): Although Justice Stevens is vague on this, he is probably referring to intervening decisional, rather than statutory, developments. The Prima Paint case, which is discussed in several of the opinions, and especially Justice O'Connor's, is an example of a major intervening decisional development. That case applied a rule (which the majority in Keating now characterizes as "procedural," but which Justice Black, dissenting in Prima Paint, labelled "substantive), which it derived from the FAA. If this type of case is what Justice Stevens means when he refers to "intervening developments in the law," the question still remains he should be bound by what he is convinced was Congress' original intention.

If Prima Paint had been unambiguous on the procedure-substance question, one could argue that Congress could have revised the statute to clarify its intentions, if it believed that the Supreme Court had misinterpreted them when it decided Prima Paint. Congress' failure to do so might then be regarded as indicating agreement with the Court's interpretation of the FAA in Prima Paint or at least a willingness to accept that interpretation, despite its own belief that the FAA was originally intended to govern only certain procedural questions related to arbitration, and then only in the federal courts, as asserted by Justice O'Connor. Congressional failure to overrule Prima Paint's interpretation would justify Justice Stevens' quoted statement.

However, the ambiguousness of the analytical basis of Prima Paint may have explained congressional inaction with respect to that decision. For all one knows, members of Congress, to the extent they thought about the matter at all, may have regarded Prima Paint as resting solely on the FAA's conferral of the right to decide certain procedural questions that arise in federal courts in FAA cases. In that event, congressional silence could hardly justify Justice Stevens' position, which, in effect, says that Justice O'Connor is correct in her reading of the FAA's scope, but that "intervening developments" require him to agree with the majority on this point.

Note 3 (Page 348): Justice O'Connor's dissenting opinion makes clear that Prima Paint had already held that the FAA could be applied in federal court diversity actions. In Bernhardt the FAA was inapplicable only because there had been no showing of a contract involving commerce. If such a showing had been made, however, the FAA would have applied. There would then have been no reason to be concerned about the "outcome determinative" test of York and Bernhardt. In short, Keating is distinguishable from Bernhardt, and does not overrule that case.

Note 4 (Page 348): In footnote 6 of the majority opinion, Chief Justice Burger states: "The procedures to be used in an arbitration are not prescribed by the federal Act. We note, however, that Prima Paint, supra, considered the question of what issues are for the courts and what issues are for the arbitrator." On the other hand, Justice O'Connor criticizes the majority for mandating "specific performance" of the arbitration agreement under the authority allegedly granted by § 2, rather than allowing the state to devise its own procedures for enforcing the arbitration agreement. Significantly, the majority does not respond to this argument of Justice O'Connor's.

One possible reading of Chief Justice Burger's statement in footnote 6 is that the courts are authorized by the FAA to decide procedural questions that are not directly dealt with in the Act--if the answers to those questions can fundamentally affect the purpose and scope of the FAA. Under such a reading, were the Court to decide in a federal court case that class-action arbitrations do have that effect, it could invalidate FAA-governed class-action arbitrations in a state court proceeding.

As for the substantive issue of whether class-action arbitrations should be permitted, this is still an open question. One argument against allowing them is that they would inevitably be more time-consuming than individual arbitrations, thus defeating one of the central goals of arbitration, speed of adjudication. On the other hand, an argument in favor of class-action arbitrations, aside from those mentioned in footnote 4 of the Court's opinion, is that the potential economies of scale will generally outweigh the financial and other costs that may be caused by a delay in resolving the dispute.

Note 5 (Page 348): Despite the widespread adoption of state arbitration statutes and the existence of the FAA, enforcement of arbitration promises is still disallowed for a variety of public policy reasons, expressed in statutes or in common law doctrine. Those policies, and related reasons for refusing to enforce an arbitration agreement, are examined in Section F of this Chapter. The state statute in *Keating*, which was interpreted by the California Supreme Court as not permitting a party to a franchise agreement to substitute arbitration for a judicial trial of certain disputes, is an example of legislation that addresses this question. Another is the federal Securities Act of 1933, the subject of *Wilko v. Swan*, which is discussed in the various opinions in *Keating* and is reported at page 410 of the Casebook.

As for Justice Stevens' position, several points can be made. The first concerns the majority's reading of the language in Section 2 that makes certain arbitration agreements "valid, irrevocable, and enforceable, save upon such grounds as exist at law or in equity for the revocation of any contract." The majority emphasizes the word "any" in that provision, and notes that the California statute invalidates agreements to arbitrate franchise agreement disputes only. In other words, it is the very selectivity of the California legislation which invalidates it. The majority also distinguishes *Wilko v. Swan*'s result on the ground that the Securities Act of 1933 was a *federal* statute, whereas the one in Keating is a state statute. Since it was Congress that enacted the FAA, its decision to limit its operation, expressed in a later congressional statute, must be respected. Such respect, implies the majority, is not owed to a state statute that undermines the federal policy favoring the enforcement of arbitration agreements in contracts involving commerce. Nor is the state policy validated by its selectivity and the state's strong public policy interests. Indeed, as noted above, its selectivity may have proved to be its undoing. It should also be noted that, ironically perhaps, some of the reasons the state had for not permitting franchise disputes to be arbitrated were highly reminiscent of reasons historically advanced against the enforcement of arbitration agreements generally, notwithstanding the state's overall receptiveness to arbitration as an institution, as evidenced by its own progressive arbitration act.

TEXTILE WORKERS UNION v. LINCOLN MILLS (Page 349)

This is a landmark case in the area of federal jurisdiction, as well as in the fields of labor relations and arbitration. On its face, Section 301(a) of the LMRA appears to be nothing more than a jurisdictional statute. It confers jurisdiction upon federal courts, without regard to diversity of citizenship or the amount in controversy, to hear suits seeking enforcement of collective bargaining agreements in commerce. If that was all that Congress intended by the statute, there would be a serious question as to whether, with respect to the absence of a diversity requirement, the jurisdictional grant exceeded Article III's limitations on federal judicial power--an issue developed in the omitted portion of Justice Frankfurter's dissenting opinion. Despite the statute's plain language, however, the Court quotes snippets from the legislative record to support its holding that Congress really intended the statute to authorize the courts to "fashion a body of federal law for the enforcement of these collective bargaining agreements and includes within that federal law specific performance of promises to arbitrate grievances under collective bargaining agreements."

NOTES AND PROBLEMS FOR DISCUSSION (Page 356)

Note 1 (Page 356): The answer to this question may seem obvious, but many students will have difficulty with it. As noted above, the federal common law principle created by the Court in Lincoln Mills was: Specific performance of promises to arbitrate grievances under collective bargaining agreements can be granted in § 301(a) suits, regardless of what the law might otherwise require in the absence of § 301(a).

Note 2 (Page 356): The "advancing lifelessness of the [Federal Arbitration] Act in labor arbitration" is a colorful and probably apt characterization of what is occuring in this area. There also will be many situations in which, though the contract being sued upon is a collective bargaining agreement, the underlying rights being asserted are those of employees under invidual hiring contracts, as described in the cited excerpt from J.I. Case Co. Arguably, such contracts would clearly be between a "class of workers engaged in foreign or interestate commerce" and their employers, and would, therefore, be outside the coverage of the FAA.

Note 4 (Page 360): City of Milwaukee's explanation of Lincoln Mills' jurisdictional basis is worth discussing. In a way, it tracks the reasoning of the Court in Erie v. Tompkins. In Erie, the Court held that the word "laws" in the Rules of Decision Act should be read as including the decisional law of the states' highest courts as well as state statutes. Without expressly acknowledging that it was doing so, Lincoln Mills read the word "laws" in Article III ("The judicial power shall extend to all cases, in law and equity, arising under this Constitution, the laws of the United States, and treaties made, or which shall be made, under their authority * * *") as including federal common law as well as federal statutes.

Note 5 (Page 360): In Keating, the majority does not say that the FAA authorizes the courts to create a body of substantive federal common law governing arbitrations under that Act. Rather, in discussing Moses H.Cone Memorial Hospital, it quotes the statement from that case that "the Arbitration Act creates a body of federal substantive law." This clearly refers to what the Act itself creates--and not to what it authorizes the courts to create. Even here, however, the majority states that not all provisions of the FAA create substantive law that is binding on state courts. Thus, in footnote 10, it emphasizes that §§ 3 and 4 of the Act do not apply to proceedings in state courts.

On the other hand, the Court states in footnote 6 that, although the FAA does not prescribe "procedures in an arbitration, Prima Paint considered the question of what issues are for the courts and what issues are for the arbitrator." The suggestion here is that the courts are authorized by the Act to decide questions that are not directly dealt with in the Act, if the answers to those questions can have important effects on the FAA's operation. This may open the door not only to consideration of other procedures with a similar effect, but also to questions of substantive law that may affect the purpose and scope of the FAA.

In either case, however, this is a far cry from the open-ended invitation to create a body of federal common law governing the enforcement of collective bargaining agreements which the Court in Lincoln Mills discerned in Congress' enactment of Section 301(a) of the LMRA. However, Justice Stevens' opinion in Keating, fails to recognize this distinction. He notes the language in § 2 of the FAA which provides that arbitration agreements are subject to revocation on such grounds as exist at law or in equity for the revocation of any contract. He then states: "The Act, however, does not define what grounds for revocation may be permissible, and hence it would appear that the judiciary must fashion the limitations as a matter of federal common law. Cf. Textile Workers v. Lincoln Mills, 353 U.S. 448, 77 S.Ct. 912, 1 L.Ed.2d 972 (1957)" Significantly, Justice Stevens employs the "Cf." signal when citing Lincoln Mills. For in the latter case, the federal courts (and later the state courts in Lucas Flour, see below) were given great latitude, circumscribed only by "the policy of our national labor laws," in fashioning federal common law principles governing the enforcement of collective bargaining agreements in commerce. (While the text and purposes of the National Labor Relations Act, which was part of the Labor Management Relations Act, was a primary source of standards for such common law principles, it was by no means the only one.) By contrast, while what Stevens urges in Keating may be characterized as the "fashioning of federal common law" under the FAA, it is probably much more appropriate to refer to it as traditional court interpretation of a statute's meaning. Again, this is significantly different from the kind of court function authorized in Lincoln Mills and its progeny.

LOCAL 174, TEAMSTERS v. LUCAS FLOUR CO. (Page 360)

An underlying problem in this case is that of federal labor law preemption. That question is examined to some extent in Vaca v. Sipes, reported at page 525 of the Casebook. However, the seminal case on this subject is San Diego Building Trades Council, etc. v. Garmon, cited in footnote 9 of the majority opinion. Garmon held that a cause of action for damages against a union for its picketing was preempted by federal labor law, i.e., that the state court had no jurisdiction to entertain such an action. The Garmon rule was stated as follows: "When it is clear or may fairly be assumed that the activities which a State purports to regulate are protected by § 7 of the National Labor Relations Act, or constitute an unfair labor practice under § 8, due regard for the federal enactment requires that state jurisdiction must yield." 359 U.S. at 244. Elsewhere in Garmon, the Court noted the underpinnings of the preemption rule. "In determining the extent to which state regulation must yield to subordinating federal authority, we have been concerned with delimiting areas of potential conflict; potential conflict of rules of law, of remedy, and of administration." Id. at 241-42. Because the "primary" jurisdiction of the National Labor Relations Board (the agency established by Congress to administer the NLRA in the first instance), plays a major role in the preemption doctrine, state and federal courts are also preempted from exercising jurisdiction when the activity is "arguably prohibited or protected" by the NLRA.

Garmon itself recognized two important exceptions to its own rule: "[D]ue regard for the presuppositions of our embracing federal system, including the principle of diffusion of power not as a matter of doctrinaire localism but as a promoter of democracy, has required us not to find withdrawal from the States of power to regulate where the activity regulated was a merely peripheral concern of the Labor Management Relations Act. See International Ass'n of Machinists v. Gonzales, 356 U.S. 617, 78 S.Ct. 923, 2 L.Ed.2d 1018. Or where the regulated conduct touched intersts so deeply rooted in local feeling and responsibility that, in the absence of compelling congressional direction, we could not infer that Congress had deprived the States of the power to act." Id. at 243-44.

The Garmon rule has been modified somewhat in later cases. The most important of these is Sears, Roebuck & Co. v. San Diego County District Council of Carpenters, 436 U.S. 180, 98 S.Ct. 1745, 56 L.Ed.2d 209 (1978). In Sears, the Court held that if an activity was merely "arguably" protected under the NLRA, and there was a strong likelihood that it was not protected in fact, the states could regulate it. The reason for this decision was that the NLRB and the courts (reviewing NLRB decisions) could determine whether the activity was protected only if an aggrieved employee or union filed a charge with the NLRB against an employer. If they did not file such a charge, and the employer were denied access to a judicial forum, no resolution of the issue could be obtained.

When it enacted § 301 in 1947, Congress itself allowed federal courts to entertain suits for breaches of collective bargaining agreements in commerce. Although such a breach is not an unfair labor practice by itself, conduct involved in the breach may be such. § 301, therefore, represents a congressional exception to the preemption rule. Because the jurisdiction conferred upon the federal courts by § 301 merely supplements the pre-existing jurisdiction of the state courts, they too may entertain such actions without violating the pre-emption principle. That is one of the principal holdings of Lucas Flour.

Although the Court holds that the state court was not barred by the preemption doctrine from entertaining the action for breach of the collective bargaining agreement, it also holds that the state court is bound to apply federal common law principles in deciding such cases. The Court does not say this in so many words, but it is also clear that, if a federal common law rule governing the matter in dispute has not been promulgated by the federal courts, the state courts have the obligation to do so. At first blush, this seems startling. Upon reflection, however, it is clear that the process is not unique to this area, especially when one recalls that state courts have often interpreted federal constitutional principles before federal courts have done so. In Loving v. Virginia, for example, 388 U.S.1, 87 S.Ct. 1817, 18 L.Ed.2d 1010 (1967), the United States Supreme Court held that a state statute criminalizing interracial marriages violated the due process and equal protection guarantees of the Fourteenth Amendment. A similar result with respect to its own state's anti-miscegenation statute had been reached by the California Supreme Court 19 years earlier in Perez v. Sharp, 32 Cal.2d 711, 198 P.2d 17 (1948).) This is a type of common law promulgation of federal constitutional principles by means of interpretation. Of course, state court decisions on the federal constitution are subject to review and "correction" by the United States Supreme Court. The same is true, however, with regard to any federal common law rules a state court might promulgate under the burden thrust upon it by Lucas Flour.

The third holding in Lucas Flour is that, pursuant to the federal common law promulgated under § 301, a union impliedly agrees not to strike over any matter that is made subject to arbitration under the collective bargaining agreement, even though the agreement does not expressly commit the union not to strike over such matters.

NOTES AND PROBLEMS FOR DISCUSSION (Page 366)

Note 1 (Page 366): Questions of interpretation involve disputes as to the meaning of contract language. Questions of application essentialy involve factual disputes. For example, suppose the labor contract provides, as most do, that the employer shall not discharge an employee except for "just cause." What is meant by "just cause" is a question of interpretation. Because of what might be described as the common law of labor arbitration based on thousands of arbitral awards, both published and unpublished, it is clear that an employee's theft of his or her employer's property, barring any extenuating circumstances, constitutes just cause for discharge. However, the employee and union may have taken the position that the employee did not in fact steal any property from the employer. This is essentially a factual dispute, one involving the "application" of the contract to particular facts. In *Lucas Flour*, the contract expressly waived the right of the union to strike in support of its position in an "interpretation" dispute. No such express waiver of the right to strike appeared, however, in the other clause which dealt with the "application" of the contract. Nevertheless, the Court infers such a no-strike promise if the matter that is struck over is made subject to arbitration by the contract.

Note 2 (Page 366): The answer appears in the last Note, and in the discussion of the case.

Note 3 (Page 366): *Carbon Fuel Co.* rejected the employer's arguments that the International Union should be held liable for a "wildcat" strike when it did not make all reasonable efforts to prevent or terminate it. The decision was based on the legislative history of §§ 301(b) and (e), and the details of the bargaining history between the union and the employer.

Hoosier Cardinal Corp. held that a uniform limitations period should not be created for pure § 301 suits, since the parties' ability to reach an agreement would not be adversely affected by having different state limitations apply. This was in contrast to the situation in *Lucas Flour* where the ability to reach an agreement would be hampered if different substantive rules were applicable in state and federal courts. (In comparing the two cases, it is instructive to examine Justice Harlan's concurring opinion in Hanna v. Plumer, 380 U.S. 460, 85 S.Ct. 1136, 14 L.Ed.2d 8 (1965). In the face of a Guaranty Trust v. York "outcome determination" challenge, Hanna v. Plumer upheld compliance with FRCP Rule 4(d)(1)'s service of process procedure in a federal court suit where jurisdiction was based on diversity of citizenship. Justice Harlan, however, disapproved of what he characterized as the Court's "arguably procedural, *ergo* constitutional" test. In its place, he preferred one that explored the effect of the rule's application "on the primary stages of private activity" which the states could regulate.)

By contrast, Del Costello applied a uniform six month limitations period, derived from the National Labor Relations Act, in the "hybrid" type suit described in the Note.

Under John Wiley & Sons, a "successor" employer has a duty to arbitrate grievances of his predecessor's employees where the successor's business is essentially a continuation of the predecessor's and the successor has hired a majority (actually 100% in John Wiley itself) of the predecessor's employees. By contrast, where the new owner has hired only a minority of the former owner's employees, this destroys the "continuity of identity" element, and the new employer is not bound by the former employer's arbitration obligation. So held Howard Johnson.

All these cases illustrate federal common law principles that have been developed by the Supreme Court under the authority it discerned in § 301 when it decided Lincoln Mills.

Note 4 (Page 367): The California Supreme Court observed in Graham v. Scissor Tail that "this court is in any event under no obligation to follow federal lower court precedents interpreting acts of Congress when we find those precedents unpersuasive. 'Any rule which require the state courts to follow in all cases the decisions of one or more lower federal courts would be undesirable, as it would have the effect of binding the state courts where neither the reasoning nor the number of federal cases is found persuasive. Such a rule would not significantly promote uniformity in federal law, for the interpretation of an act of Congress by a lower federal court does not bind other federal courts except those directly subordinate to it. [Citations.]' (Rohr Aircraft Corp. v. County of San Diego (1959) 51 Cal.2d 759, 764-765 [336 P.2d 521], revd. without comment on this point, 362 U.S. 628 [4 L.Ed.2d 1002, 80 S.Ct. 1050] * * *"

D. DIVISION OF AUTHORITY BETWEEN COURTS AND ARBITRATORS (Page 367)

ERICKSEN, ARBUTHNOT, McCARTHY, KEARNEY & WALSH, INC. v. 100 OAK STREET (Page 367)

The problem in this case, as in Prima Paint, is a mind-boggler. If a contract has been induced by fraud, it would appear that none of the provisions of the contract would be valid, including the arbitration provision, and that a court, rather than an arbitrator, should, therefore, determine in the first place whether the contract was induced by fraud. However, because of the strong contemporary legislative and judicial policies favoring arbitration--how different from the attitudes of the past!--most courts that have considered the question have held that the arbitration clause is separable from the rest of the contract. In their view, fraud may be entirely absent from the agreement to arbitrate, although it permeates everything else in the contract. Those courts frankly acknowledge that an interest in relieving judicial burdens is a prime factor in how they resolve this problem. Like Ericksen, the overwhelming majority of courts hold that, if they do not determine that the agreement to arbitrate was induced by fraud, it is up to the arbitrator to decide whether the contract as a whole was so induced. Implicit in this holding is the principle, explained in greater detail in later cases, that whether the parties have agreed to arbitrate at all, or to arbitrate particular kinds of questions, is for the courts to decide--although, insofar as particular kinds of disputes are concerned, the arbitrator may decide whether they are arbitrable if the parties have clearly expressed their intention in the contract that he or she do so.

NOTES AND PROBLEMS FOR DISCUSSION (Page 379)

Note 1 (Page 379): In Ericksen, the court distinguishes state court cases that are governed by the FAA from those that are governed by a state arbitration statute. That is evident from its separate examination of "The Federal Rule" and "The Rule in Other States." Also, in discussing the New York Court of Appeals' reasons for revising its state rule to bring it into harmony with the federal rule of Prima Paint, Judge Grodin states: "An 'additional and desirable result' of its decision, the New York court notes, was to bring that state's law in accord with federal law as declared in Prima Paint, thus avoiding the awkwardness of applying different rules depending upon whether the case involved a contract subject to the federal statute. '[I]t is a rather technical distinction to apply one law or another depending on whether interstate commerce is involved.'" These statements suggest that if the contract in question evidences "a transaction involving commerce," the Prima Paint rule would have to be applied by a state court. If the contract did not affect commerce, however, the FAA would not apply and a state could ignore the federal rule allocating decision-making authority between arbitrators and courts in this sort of case. If there was ever any doubt that such would be the result, they were dispelled by the result and rationale of Keating.

If the contract merely "affects" commerce, but is not "a contract evidencing a transaction involving commerce," whether it is covered by the FAA must be determined. Because it has been defined as not being "a contract evidencing a transaction involving commerce," it would appear at first blush to be outside the scope of the FAA, given that language in the Act. Recall, however, the court's emphasis in Bernhardt that the party who sought to invoke the FAA had failed to "make a showing" that he was "working 'in commerce,' was producing goods for commerce, or was engaging in activity that affected commerce, within the meaning of our decisions." (Emphasis supplied.) This would suggest that, despite the literal language of the FAA, a contract that merely "affects" commerce would be covered by the Act.

As for the removal of a state case to a federal district court on grounds of diversity of citizenship, it would appear, on the basis of Prima Paint and Keating, that the rima Paint rule could be applied by the federal court if the contract in question were also governed by the FAA, i.e., if the state court itself would have had to apply the Prima Paint rule, but not if it were governed by state arbitration law. (Recall the Keating majority's rejection of the argument that the FAA merely governs procedure in the federal courts.

Note 2 (Page 380): A tenable rationalization of the cases is that: 1) Prima Paint merely represents an interpretation of explicit provisions of the FAA, rather than the promulgation of a federal common law rule; 2) Keating merely requires state courts to apply those explicit provisions to contracts otherwise covered by the statute.

Note 3 (Page 381): If an arbitration clause is separable from the rest of a contract, as the majorities in Prima Paint and Ericksen held, the only inquiry a court should make is whether the inclusion of that clause was induced by fraud. If it was not, the person who is ordered to arbitrate cannot be said to have been "forced" to "forgo his opportunity to try his legal issues in the courts." According to the court's finding, he or she voluntarily agreed to the resolution of contract-related disputes by an arbitrator rather than a court.

COUNTRY MUTUAL INSURANCE COMPANY v. KOSMOS (Page 381)

NOTES AND PROBLEMS FOR DISCUSSION (Page 384)

Note 1 (Page 384): In its basic holding, this case is consistent with Ericksen and Prima Paint. Those cases held or implied that whether the parties had agreed to arbitrate was for a court to decide; and that if the court answered the question in the affirmative the arbitrator was free to rule that there had been fraud in the inducement with respect to the rest of the contract. In Kosmos also, the court holds that whether the parties had agreed to arbitrate is a judicial question. Reading the arbitration clause and the pleadings, it concludes that this dispute is not arbitrable because neither party had alleged that there had been physical contact between another vehicle and the insured's. Moreover, the court interprets the concededly ambiguous language of the 1978 statutory amendment, and concludes that it was not intended "to extend the scope of arbitration." It is significant that the court does not discuss whether there is a "presumption of arbitrability," the subject that is explored in the following section of the Casebook. As will be seen there, such a presumption exists in the labor field, and, with some exceptions, has also been adopted in commercial arbitration. That presumption, however, applies only with respect to interpreting the intentions of the parties; it does not apply with respect to the interpretion of legislative intentions as expressed in statutes.

Fruchtman held that "the coverage dispute was not arbitrable under the policy definition of a 'hit-and-run vehicle,' requiring 'physical contact' with such vehicle as a precondition to coverage and the unrefuted fact disclosed by the record that there was no such contact." 263 N.W.2d at 68. In Benson, the court stated the issue as "whether, under the arbitration clause of an uninsured motorist endorsement, the question of the existence of a 'phantom' hit and run driver should be decided by a court, as a preliminary matter, or by an arbitrator." 432 Atl. at 906. It held that, under the policy in the case, the issue was not a question for the court, "but one, together with issues of negligence and damages, for the arbitrator." Id.

As the quoted excerpts indicate, American arbitrators are permitted to decide law, as well as fact, questions. They may do so, however, only after it has been determined, by a court or by the parties' acquiescence, that they have jurisdiction to decide a particular dispute or disputes. If that preliminary question is decided by a court, however, and if its answer depends upon a construction of law, as in Kosmos, it would be improper, if not unconstitutional (as the court suggests) to refer that law question to an arbitrator over the objections of one of the parties.

E. PRESUMPTIONS ABOUT ARBITRABILITY (Page 384)

UNITED STEELWORKERS v. AMERICAN MANUFACTURING CO. (Page 384)

The question of substantive arbitrability which courts are often called upon to decide is divisible into two subsidiary questions. One is whether the parties had agreed to arbitrate at all. Even if the answer to that question is yes, a court may still have to decide whether the parties had agreed to arbitrate the particular type of dispute now dividing the parties. The first question is explored at length in the next section of this chapter. Although courts often must answer it before examining the second question, these subject areas are examined in reverse order in the Casebook. This was deemed desirable because of the internal case references in each group of cases. Moreover, as in the cases in this section, in many, if not most, instances, the "first" question--whether the parties agreed to arbitrate at all--is not in issue.

American Manufacturing and the other two cases of the _Steelworkers' Trilogy_, (the next case, _Warrior & Gulf Mfg._, and _Enterprise Wheel_, reported at page 744 of the Casebook, in the section on Judicial Review of Arbitration Awards) establish a strong presumption of arbitrability of disputes arising under collective bargaining agreements that contain arbitration provisions. (Over 95% do contain such provisions.) In _American Manufacturing_, the Court emphasizes that the policy of Section 203(d) of the Labor Management Relations Act "can be effectuated only if the means chosen by the parties for settlement of their differences under a collective bargaining agreement is given full play." As a result, the "function of the court is very limited when the parties have agreed to submit questions of contract interpretation to the arbitrator. It is confined to ascertaining whether the party seeking arbitration is making a claim which on its face is governed by the contract."

The import of the case can be highlighted as follows: Suppose the collective agreement had not contained an arbitration clause, but was the same in all other respects. Suppose further that the injured employee was discharged by the employer, and sued the employer for breach of the collective bargaining agreement. If the employer were to move for summary judgment on the basis of affidavits establishing the facts as related in _American Manufacturing_, the motion could be granted, and might very well survive an appeal. In any event, it would be within the trial court's province to decide that, in view of the contract language and the medical determination, the plaintiff's claim was frivolous (although, as will be seen below, that is arguable in any event). By contrast, when the collective agreement contains an arbitration clause, even though the court evaluates the grievant's claim in the same way, it may not decide the merits of the dispute. The parties bargained for an arbitrator to do this, and are bound by their choice. For the same reasons, it makes no difference that the arbitrator's decision is different from how the court would have decided the case.

NOTES AND PROBLEMS FOR DISCUSSION (Page 387)

Note 1 (Page 387): The class might first explore precisely what "therapeutic values" can be found in the "processing of even frivolous claims." Employees and employers will generally continue their basic relationship long after they resolve particular disputes. In addition, the employer and the union leadership both have constituencies--shareholders in the employer's case and union members, or, more precisely, members of the bargaining unit represented by the union, in the union's case--whose continued allegience and respect have to be preserved. To be sure, arbitrators will presumably rule against claimants whose grievances, they find, are frivolous. Nevertheless, the opportunity to present those grievances for decision by an impartial third-party, to vent frustrations, whether justified or not, to know that one has had the equivalent of a day in court, can all serve to ensure future harmony not only between the aggrieved employee and the employer, but also between the employee and his or her union representatives. Of course, where the penalty upheld by the arbitrator is the employee's discharge, the equation is changed somewhat. But even here, the effect on the remaining employees who know that this process has occurred is often therapeutic for the same reasons.

As for the specific question posed in this Note, a labor arbitrator could reasonably decide that, under the circumstances of American Mfg., the employee's discharge was not for "just cause." The workers' compensation determination that the employee is 25% permanently partially disabled is arguably not the same as a finding that the employee is 25% less able to perform the particular job he or she had been performing prior to the disabling injury.

UNITED STEELWORKERS OF AMERICA v. WARRIOR & GULF NAVIGATION CO. (Page 387)

This case is important not only for its elaboration of the "presumption of arbitrability" and related principles in cases governed by the Labor Management Relations Act, but also because of its exploration of the labor arbitrator's special role. As for the first point, the principles evolved in this case are additional "federal common law" rules created by the Court under the _Lincoln Mills_ doctrine. Those principles are best summarized in Justice Whittaker's dissenting opinion: 1) The labor arbitrator's source of law is "not confined to the express provisions of the contract." 2) "Doubts of [arbitrability] should be resolved in favor of coverage." 3) When "an absolute no-strike clause is included in the agreement, then * * * everything that management does is subject to [arbitration]." The last principle is analogous to the one enunciated in _Lucas Flour_, that a union may not strike over matters made arbitrable by the contract, although the contract does not contain an express no-strike pledge.

As for the labor arbitrator's special role, a strong argument can be made that the Court blurs the distinction between rights and interests arbitration. All three cases of the Trilogy concern grievance ("rights") arbitration. As will be recalled, the generally recognized function of the arbitrator in such cases is to decide questions of interpretation and application of contract terms previously agreed to by the parties--and not to write new terms for them. Yet there is much in the Court's language that suggests that, in engaging in grievance arbitration, the arbitrator may in fact write terms for the parties. The Court recognizes that the collective bargaining agreement cannot cover every contingency, that it will have gaps in it that will have to be filled by the arbitrator, that in performing this function the arbitrator may look to the "common law of the shop and the industry," and that the arbitrator's resolution of these disputes is part and parcel of the bargaining process. In many ways, this is reminiscent of the role of judges in a common law judicial system. Even where much of the law has been codified by a legislature, the courts create substantive rules in the course of interpreting and applying statutes to specific situations, subject to "overruling" by subsequent legislation.

One of the observations in Justice Brennan's concurring opinion is especially relevant to the above comments. He notes that the lower courts "found that _Warrior_ was in no way limited by any _implied_ covenants of good faith and fair dealing from contracting out as it pleased." The fact is that many arbitrators have held that, despite a collective bargaining agreement's silence on the right of the employer to "contract out" unit work, such a limitation can be found in the contract's implied covenant of good faith and fair dealing. Cf. Matter of Allis-Chalmers Manufacturing Co., 39 L.A. 1213 (1962) (Smith). It is submitted that such a holding is a form of "interests" arbitration in that it adds a term to the contract that is not expressly contained in it.

In determining the scope of the matters excluded from arbitration by the "management rights" clause, it is clear that the courts may not examine the bargaining history that led to the adoption of that clause. Less clear is whether the courts may look at other provisions of the contract that might shed some light on the meaning of that clause, if those other provisions are brought to their attention by one or both parties. Once the court does this, it would appear to be invading the province of the arbitrator, since those other provisions more often than not will have to be interpreted. The court's position would be weaker still if it scoured the contract on its own initiative to find language that might identify the subjects that were intended to be excluded from arbitration by the "management rights" clause.

NOTES AND PROBLEMS FOR DISCUSSION (Page 398)

Note 2 (Page 398): Some responses to Judge Hays' criticisms of labor arbitration: 1) The task that Congress entrusted to the judiciary with respect to the collective bargaining agreement was not to fashion the law governing "it," but rather to fashion the law governing "its enforcement"--at least as suggested by *Lincoln Mills*. There is a world of difference in these two concepts; 2) Although particular arbitrators may know nothing of the common law of the shop or the industry, the likelihood is that judges will know even less. On the other hand, many, if not most arbitrators, by virtue of their training, experience and continued exposure to labor cases, can and do develop a sensitivity to the underlying elements of labor-management relations that the Court regarded as important in *Warrior & Gulf*; 3) Many judges are not especially well equipped for the judicial task. Also, parties, who voluntarily select arbitrators, are generally aware of any limitations they may have in this respect. In addition, many arbitrators are lawyers, law professors, or otherwise trained in the law. A perusal of the various collections of published arbitration awards (e.g., CCH Labor Arbitration Awards; BNA Labor Arbitration Reports) will find opinions whose quality of reasoning and result is equal, if not superior, to many judicial decision; 4) That the arbitrator must be jointly selected by union and employer militates against arbitral bias. In most situations, however, there is a greater statistical likelihood that an arbitrator will be doing business with a particular union (or firm of union attorneys) than with a particular employer. For example, suppose Attorney Firm A represents 15 unions, each of which has collective bargaining agreements with 30 employers. While some of those employers may be represented by the same firm of attorneys, most will have separate lawyers. If the arbitrator decides a case against a union, he runs the risk of displeasing that union's attorney who then has the power to exclude him from consideration as arbitrator in disputes involving 450 employers. On the other hand, if the arbitrator rules in favor of the union, he may displease the single employer or employer's attorney involved in that case, but the likelihood of widespread repercussions in that event is remote. Another potential weakness of labor arbitration is that arbitrators would be naturally chary of consistently deciding in favor of one side. This tempts some arbitrators to try to please both parties in an award, thereby doing justice to neither (although frequently, the issues are sufficiently numerous and complex to justify a ruling that, in different parts, favors each side). The most telling answer to these potential problems is that arbitration is a profession. Arbitrators are governed by Codes of Ethical Behavior, and take pride in their work. 5) Finally, one of the major problems with the proposed establishment of "labor courts" is that parties would sacrifice their right mutually to select the person or persons who would hear and determine their disputes. Also, it is not clear that the "labor courts," where they exist in Europe, have been especially successful.

Comparing Judge Hays' criticisms of labor arbitration with Judge Story's reservations about arbitration in general, one can discern certain similarities. Above all, each is persuaded that arbitration represents second-hand justice, lacking the procedural safeguards and facilities of judicial trials. What each seems to overlook is that this form of adjudication is voluntarily chosen by the parties, and that, with its speed, privacy, and relative inexpensivenesss, it offers many positive advantages. Especially in the labor field, where, as the Court observed in Warrior & Gulf, arbitration is not only a substitute for litigation, but also a substitute for industrial warfare, there is much to recommend it.

Note 3 (Page 399): The article by Professors Smith and Jones indicates that, although arbitrators may generally decide any issues properly before them, including arbitrability of a grievance, some arbitrators have treated American Manufacturing and Warrior & Gulf as precluding them from deciding the types of arbitrability issues decided in those cases. They conclude as follows:

"Actually, we believe it makes no difference in cases like these whether an arbitrator holds the grievance arbitrable and then denies it on the merits (if this should be his conclusion) or dismisses it as non-arbitrable. Either form of decision would have to be predicated on the same basic contractual analysis, namely, that there is no provision in the labor agreement which supports the grievance. The legal and practical results are, therefore, the same, and the point of the matter is that either way the arbitrator writes his opinion he is in fact deciding the merits. For this reason, we doubt that the Court would upset an arbitrator's holding of non-arbitrability." 65 Mich. L. Rev. at 761.

But what if the arbitrator decides that the grievance is meritorious as well as arbitrable?

BOWMER v.BOWMER (Page 400)

The majority opinion appears to misapply the familiar maxim, "expressio unius, exclusio alterius est." If the references in the arbitration clause had been restricted to the items specifically made arbitrable in other parts of the agreement, the majority opinion would be more supportable. (Even then, one could ask what purposes were served by the special arbitration clause if all it did was to incorporate the contract's other arbitration provisions.) The inescapable conclusion, as the dissent emphasizes, is that the generalized arbitration clause means what it says, namely that it applies to, among other things, "[a]ny claim, dispute or misunderstanding arising out of or in connection with this Agreement * * * ."

NOTES AND PROBLEMS FOR DISCUSSION (Page 407)

Note 1 (Page 407): The restrictive reading the majority gives to this broad arbitration clause appears inconsistent with the principles it developed in the Weinrott case, as well as with its recognition that parties could expressly confer upon an arbitrator the authority to reduce alimony payments in the light of changed circumstances. As indicated in the above discussion of the case, however, Bowmer appears to rely on a strained reading of the specific provisions of this contract, exaggerating the significance of the arbitration clause's reference to other arbitration promises in the contract, and emphasizing the contract's detailed and flexible formula for computing alimony. Once again, despite both of these features of the contract, the arbitration clause's meaning appears to be clear on its face. One can only speculate that, despite its previous recognition that parties may authorize arbitrators to modify alimony obligations on the basis of changed circumstances, the court is not too comfortable with that rule, and is seeking to limit it where it can, as in the present case.

Note 2 (Page 407): If one is referring to grievance arbitration in the public sector, i.e., where it revolves around the alleged breach of a collective bargaining agreement, the notion of non-delegability of a public function by the public employer seems misplaced. Without arbitration, grievance disputes could be resolved by the employer in one of two ways. It could compromise its position in response to an illegal strike by its employees in support of the grievant. In addition, the grievant or union could sue for breach of the contract, or the employer could seek a judicial declaration that it had not breached the contract. Under any of these scenarios, the decision would be delegated to a third party, namely a court. When arbitration is invoked, the character of the third party decision-maker is changed, but the underlying principle remains the same.

Different considerations are present in interests arbitration, however, since neither public employers, unions nor employees may invoke the aid of the courts to determine the terms a contract should contain. As will be seen in Dearborn Firefighters, reported at page 844 of the Casebook, the problem of whether a public employer has delegated a non-delegable duty is difficult and complex in the area of public-sector interests arbitration. The main concern is that, by referring such matters to arbitrators, public officials can avoid public accountability. They can, in effect, say: "It was not us who gave this generous increase in salaries to our employees (which caused an increase in your taxes), but the arbitrator who did it." To some extent, and without constitutional implications, a similar problem of accountability exists in the private sector. A corporation's shareholders, for example, will be concerned with the contracts concluded between their corporate officers and the unions they bargain with.

F. HAVE THE PARTIES ENTERED INTO A VALID AGREEMENT, AND ARE THEY NOW BOUND BY IT? (Page 410)

1. DOES THE AGREEMENT VIOLATE PUBLIC POLICY? (Page 410)

WILKO v. SWAN (Page 410)

Despite the clear and unequivocal promise to arbitrate here and its coverage by the FAA (enacted in 1925), the Court holds that the language and policy of the Securities Act of 1933 renders this arbitration agreement unenforceable. Although Congress did not expressly refer to the FAA (then United States Arbitration Act) in the Securities Act, its general invalidation of any "condition, stipulation, or provision binding any person acquiring any security to waive compliance with any provision" of the Act is interpreted as applying to an agreement to arbitrate future controversies. The main factors stressed by the Court are: 1) the choice of state or federal courts accorded by the Securities Act, with no removal being allowed; 2) the special venue privileges conferred by the Securities Act; 3) its provisions for nation-wide service of process; and 4) the impractability of effective judicial review of an arbitrator's determination of legal questions because arbitrators need not write opinions (or issue them orally) rationalizing their awards; and even if they issued such opinions, their awards could not be set aside for mere errors in interpreting the law, only for "manifest disregard of the law." (This last point is examined in detail at p. 760 et seq of the Casebook.)

Here, then, although the parties thought they were doing so at the time, they did not enter into a valid and binding arbitration agreement. It was invalidated by the strong public policy declared by the same political entity, Congress, that had previously enunciated the strong public policy favoring arbitration. (Compare Keating, in which strong public policy embodied in a state statute collided with the FAA's pro-arbitration policy in a state court case that the Court concluded was also governed by the FAA. In Keating, the Court held that the state policy should give way to the federal policy in the FAA.)

NOTES AND PROBLEMS FOR DISCUSSION (Page 416)

Note 1 (Page 416): The court concludes: "[W]hile a bankruptcy court would have the power to stay proceedings pending arbitration, the use of this power is left to the sound discretion of the bankruptcy court." Would a similar approach have been appropriate in Wilko v. Swan? That is, should the trial court in that case have been ordered to examine all the circumstances before deciding whether to grant the defendant's request for a stay pending arbitration? It would seem that the situations in these cases are distinguishable in a qualitative as well as quantitative sense. In Zimmerman, the only value to be served was that of speed and efficiency of adjudication in the bankruptcy proceeding, as a result of the Bankruptcy Reform Act's expansion of jurisdiction in the bankruptcy court. By contrast, a whole range of advantages, including an unfettered choice of tribunal, was created by the Securities Act of 1933.

Note 2 (Page 418): Moran held that the arbitrator's award would be allowed to stand under the circumstances described in the question. Recall that in _Wilko_, the Court stresses that by the agreement to arbitrate, petitioner was "restricted in his choice of forum prior to the existence of a controversy. While the Securities Act does not require petitioner to sue, a waiver in advance of a controversy stands upon a different footing." This point is stressed also in Justice Jackson's concurring opinion.

Note 3 (Page 418): If, as _Moran_ holds, parties may voluntarily submit a Securities Act dispute to arbitration pursuant to an arbitration agreement concluded before the dispute arose, then, _a fortiori_, joint submission of such a dispute is valid when it is not based on a pre-dispute agreement to do so.

DEAN WITTER REYNOLDS, INC. v. BYRD (Page 419)

The Court assumes, but does not decide, that securities claims under the Securities Exchange Act of 1934 are, like those under the Securities Act of 1933, non-arbitrable. Rejecting the position of some Courts of Appeals, it holds that when a complaint raises both non-arbitrable federal securities claims and pendent state claims (and the parties had previously agreed to arbitrate their disputes), a federal district court may not deny a motion to compel arbitration of the state-law claims. Conceding that one aim of the FAA was to expedite dispute resolution through arbitration, it stresses that the FAA's principal goal was to make arbitration promises enforceable. It also rejects the argument that the arbitration award on the state claims, if it precedes the resolution of the federal securities act case, will necessarily have a collateral estoppel effect in the federal securities act case. On this point, it notes that it had recently held in _McDonald v. City of West Branch_ that neither the federal full faith and credit statute, 28 U.S.C. § 1738, nor a judicially fashioned rule of preclusion permits "a federal court to accord res judicata or collateral-estoppel effect to an _unappealed_ arbitration award in a case brought under 42 U.S.C.§ 1983." (Emphasis supplied.)

The class should be reminded of this section's title: "Have the parties entered into a valid agreement and are they now bound by it?" In _Byrd_, garden variety state-law claims, previously made subject to arbitration by the parties' agreement, narrowly escape being rendered nonarbitrable by their close relationship to other claims that are assumed to be nonarbitrable.

The applicability of the Wilko v. Swan doctrine to §

10(b) of the Securities Exchange Act of 1934 and Rule 10(b)(5), as indicated by both the majority and the dissent, is still an open question. Only because Dean Witter did not seek to compel arbitration of the federal securities claims in the district court does the Court not resolve it here. Consideration of this question can await reading of the next case, Scherk v. Alberto Culver.

The preclusive effect of arbitration awards is examined in Section H(7) of this Chapter. For the time being, it is worth mentioning that both the FAA and state arbitration statutes modelled on the Uniform Arbitration Act contain procedures for summary judicial confirmation of arbitration awards. Once an award is confirmed, or if it is made subject to a separate suit to enforce it, a state court's resulting judgment may well be entitled to full faith and credit under 28 U.S.C. § 1738. If so, one should consider whether this would constitute an intolerable undermining of the policy enunciated in Wilko v. Swan. Stated differently, would this not mean that vital issues of a federal securities claim, which the Supreme Court has held nonarbitrable, would be decided in effect by an arbitrator?

<u>NOTES AND PROBLEMS FOR DISCUSSION</u> (Page 426)

<u>Note 1</u> (Page 426): The state-law claims in <u>Byrd</u> "derive from a common nucleus of operative fact" and, absent an arbitration provision, a plaintiff "would ordinarily be expected to try them all in one judicial proceeding." On the other hand, in view of the arbitration agreement, their subjection to court trial together with the federal securities claims would violate the "fairness to litigants" requirement for a federal court's discretionary exercise of pendent jurisdiction. It would be unfair to the defendant, Dean Witter, whose contract with the plaintiff included a provision which, as applied to the state law claims, was valid and enforceable. Staying the arbitration proceedings could also be unfair to the plaintiff if: 1) the plaintiff prevails in arbitration; 2) the award is rendered and judicially confirmed prior to the termination of the federal securities act suit; and 3) the Court ultimately rules that, under such circumstances, 28 U.S.C. § 1738 requires the federal court to give full faith and credit to the judgment confirming the arbitration award.

<u>Note 2</u> (Page 427): Based on their particular legislative histories, state arbitration statutes and state statutory causes of action that preclude arbitration could be variously interpreted by state courts. If those combined ar-

bitrable and non-arbitrable state claims are litigated in a federal court on the basis of diversity of citizenship, the Guaranty Trust v. York doctrine, as applied in Bernhardt, would require that court to apply the state law, since, as the question is stated, all the claims are "governed by state, rather than federal, law."

SCHERK v. ALBERTO-CULVER (Page 427)

As in Byrd, the Court assumes, without deciding, that the Securities Exchange Act of 1934 creates a right to refuse to abide by a promise to arbitrate disputes covered by the Act, if the promise is made in an entirely (or perhaps predominantly) domestic contract. Only because the contract here is "international" in its origins and scope does the Court hold that the Wilko rule does not apply.

The case resolves conflicting pulls and tugs. Pulling in one direction is the FAA, which encourages arbitration agreements and makes them enforceable. Pulling in an opposite direction is the policy, discerned in Wilko, of not permitting parties to waive in advance their right to a judicial tribunal to resolve federal securities claims. Finally, pulling back in the direction of permitting arbitration is the international character of the contract in Scherk, the Court's concern that the United States not strike other nations as being too parochial when it comes to recognizing international agreements to arbitrate, and the practical difficulties that would be encountered in attempting to follow the Wilko doctrine under these circumstances.

MITSUBISHI MOTORS CORP. v. SOLER CHRYSLER-PLYMOUTH, INC. (Page 431)

Before examining the contract's international aspects, one should first explore why lower federal courts have held that federal antitrust claims are nonarbitrable, despite the applicability of FAA, § 2 to the parties' contract. Unlike the Wilko principle, where the nonarbitrability of claims under the Securities Act of 1933 was based on later-enacted congressional legislation, the rule here is entirely judge-made. The reasons for the rule are set forth in the Court's characterization of American Safety's rationale. Its criticism of some aspects of that rationale suggests that in an appropriate case it might be inclined to reject the rule of that case--even in an entirely domestic setting.

Among other ways, the majority and dissent disagree on whether the contract's arbitration clause embraces the antitrust claims. Without putting its analysis in precisely these terms, the majority appears to indulge in a broad presumption of arbitrability. By contrast, the dissent, noting the strong public policies surrounding antitrust litigation, would read the clause restrictively. It also insists that, in reading the contract, the antitrust claims cannot be regarded as "a dispute 'in relation to'" the articles referred to in the arbitration clause.

In the First Circuit's decision in this case, the court considered and rejected the claim that American insistence on deciding federal antitrust claims in federal courts would be regarded as "parochial" by other nations. It noted the existence of antitrust principles in the legislation of Germany, the European Economic Community, and Japan, among other nations. "In any event," it continued, "whether or not other nations agree with United States law and attitudes relating to competition, it is extremely doubtful that they would describe them as 'parochial' in the sense of being petty provincialisms." This is an exceedingly persuasive argument. It suggests that the Court's reliance on Scherk in this case may have been misplaced, and that even the result in Scherk may have been largely based on the practical difficulties of denying the arbitration remedy in the international context, rather than the professed concern over the "parochial" image doing so might convey to other nations.

NOTES AND PROBLEMS FOR DISCUSSION (Page 461)

Note 1 (Page 461): a) Justice Stevens asserts that the arbitration clause applies only to two-party disputes between Soler and Mitsubishi, and not to a claim by Soler against Mitsubishi and Chrysler. The majority does not appear to respond to this second point, but a possible answer is that Soler's antitrust claim against Mitsubishi and Chrysler necessarily embraces a claim against Mitsubishi itself. As noted above, Justice Stevens also insists that the antitrust dispute is not one "in relation" to the Articles specified in the contract. In response to this point, the majority notes that Mitsubishi relies on particular provisions of the contract as a defense to the anti-trust claim; therefore, the dispute is embraced by the language of the arbitration clause that covers disputes "in relation to" Articles I-B through V of the Agreement. It should be noted that the scope of the phrase "in relation to" is much broader than that of "arising under" found in Article III of the federal constitution. The Supreme Court has held that the "arising under" language permits Congress to confer jurisdiction upon the federal courts over cases in which the federal element may apppear only in a defendant's responsive pleading. See Osborn v. Bank of United States, 9 Wheat. 738, 6 L.Ed. 204 (1824); cf. Textile Workers v. Lincoln Mills, 353 U.S. at 460, 77 S.Ct. at 923, 1 L.Ed.2d at 983 (1957) (Frankfurter, J., dissenting).

b) Justice Stevens says statutory remedies reflect strong public policies which can be effectively implemented only in the judicial tribunals designated by the statute in question; and that the FAA should, therefore, not be interpreted to embrace them. The majority says it will not read Section 2 of the FAA as creating a presumption against the arbitrability of claims for which special remedies are provided by statute. At first blush, the majority's position seems at odds with the principles enunciated in the cases cited by Stevens: Alexander v. Gardner-Denver; Barrentine; and McDonald. (These are examined in Section H(7) of this Chapter, dealing with the preclusive effects of arbitral awards.) However, although the majority treats this issue separately, that treatment cannot be separated from the context in which the issue arises--namely, the international character of the arbitration agreement, and the Court's special concerns about comity, practicability and "parochialism" that were stressed in Scherk. Moreover, the Court makes clear that, although an arbitration remedy may be substituted for a judicial remedy under these circumstances, it would not enforce an arbitral award if the arbitrators had refused to apply the provisions of American antitrust law to this dispute, and had applied some other law instead. See footnote 19 of Justice Blackmun's opinion.

c) Justice Stevens' main reason for concluding that Congress did not intend § 2 of the FAA to apply to federal antitrust claims is that the private plaintiff in an antitrust action is a "private attorney general" who, in a treble damage recovery, vindicates a public interest. The majority stresses that, although this may be an incidental effect of a successful private antitrust suit, the Sherman Act's primary purpose in allowing such private suits is to provide redress for individuals who have been injured by a defendant's antitrust violations. It is of some note that Justice Stevens raises this question with respect to "antitrust claims" in general, not differentiating between federal and state antitrust claims. By contrast, the majority notes that, in the light of Keating, there isn't even a colorable argument that state antitrust claims can be excluded from the FAA's declaration that arbitration agreements in commerce are "valid, irrevocable and enforceable."

d) Having concluded that the antitrust suit was not covered by the FAA, Justice Stevens also asserts that Congress did not intend the Convention to apply to such suits. He stresses that Scherk was based on the posssibility of conflict-of-laws problems, and the uncertainty such a possibility would cause. (Even the majority concedes there would be no such problem here, however. The Japanese arbitrators would have to apply Sherman Act principles to the antitrust issue in the case. If they did not, their award, the majority assures us, would not be enforced.) The majority's response to Justice Stevens' argument on this point is simply to reiterate the considerations that led to the decisions in Scherk and The Bremen: comity, parochialism, practicality, and the notion that those who engage in international transactions should, in effect, be prepared to take the heat or get out of the kitchen.

Note 2 (Page 461): As noted above, although the majority assumes the validity of the American Safety rule precluding arbitration of federal antitrust claims in an entirely domestic context, its gratuitous criticism of some aspects of the rationale of that decision suggests that it may be inclined to reject it on an appropriate occasion. Logically, American arbitrators can be trusted as much as, or more than, foreign arbitrators to apply Sherman Act principles correctly to antitrust claims they are asked by both parties to decide. However, it would be difficult for the Court to reject American Safety without overruling Blumenstock, which held that state courts could not entertain federal antitrust suits. The Court could distinguish the domestic and international situations once more by relying on the "comity, parochialism, practicality" factors.

Note 3 (Page 461): Judge Weinberg's language in American Safety stressing, as does Justice Stevens elsewhere in his opinion, the public character of what appears on the surface to be only a private matter, suggests that the concerns expressed by Professor Fiss about the practice of settlement may have considerable validity in the area of arbitration. The resolution of private antitrust or other disputes by arbitrators may slight the public interest. [Because the APPA (see United States v. Bechtel, page 202 of the Casebook) applies only to consent decrees between the Government and the antitrust defendant/s, its safeguards do not protect against an arbitration award resolving a private antitrust dispute that may ignore or harm the public interest. At the same time, it is noteworthy that even Justice Stevens tentatively approves cases distinguishing agreements to arbitrate antitrust claims after those claims arise by analogizing this to private settlement of such claims where the parties "have had every opportunity to evaluate the strength of their position."]

Note 4 (Page 461): See the last two sentences in footnote 21 of Justice Blackmun's majority opinion: "Doubtless, Congress may specify categories of claims it wishes to reserve for decision by our own courts without contravening this Nation's obligation under the Convention. But we decline to subvert the spirit of the United States' accession to the Convention by recognizing subject-matter exceptions where Congress has not expressly directed the courts to do so." (Emphasis supplied.) Thus, the Court serves notice that it will also not recognize any other judge-made subject-matter exceptions to arbitrability of issues made subject to arbitration by an international commercial arbitration agreement.

RHONE MEDITERRANEE COMPAGNIA FRANCESE DI ASSICURAZIONI E RIASSICURAZONI v. LAURO (Page 461)

NOTES AND PROBLEMS FOR DISCUSSION (Page 466)

Note 1 (Page 466): By noting that "Rhone is not faced with an Italian public policy disfavoring arbitration, but only with an Italian procedural rule of arbitration which may have been overlooked by the drafters of the time charter agreement," the court strongly implies that it would respect an Italian "law" that prohibited arbitration of insurance claims. Such a "law" would reflect a "fundamental" policy. Recall, however, *Mitsubishi Motors*' footnote 19, which announced that American judge-made rules making certain commercial claims not arbitrable would be ignored if the arbitration clause was covered by the Convention. Should an American court pay greater respect to rules developed by foreign courts than to those developed by courts in their own country? (To be sure, in civil law jurisdictions, the "law" is presumably limited to what is found in legislatively promulgated Codes. Nevertheless, because of their authority to interpret such "laws," civil law courts often perform functions that are not unlike those performed by their common law counterparts.) On the other hand, with respect to their potential effect upon international relations, isn't there a fundamental difference between an American court characterizing its own judge-made (or even, as in *Scherk*, legislature-made) law as "parochial" and pronouncing a similar judgment on a law or policy of a foreign nation? The language of Article II, Section 3 does not appear to permit the courts of a contracting contracting state to make such value judgments about the laws of other contracting states.

Note 2 (Page 466): By limiting the meaning of the words "null and void, inoperative or incapable of being performed" in Article II section 3 of the Convention, the Rhone Mediteranee court, like the Supreme Court in Mitsubishi Motors, engages in what might be described as a "presumption of arbitrability" with respect to international commercial agreements.

Note 3 (Page 466): In Rhone Mediteranee, the court was confronted with an international conflict of laws problem affected by the express language of the Convention. The problem in this Note also involves a conflict of laws question--although this time, it is a conflict between the laws of sister states in the United States. There are several ways in which the problem could be resolved. The forum court could hold that the contract violates its own strong public policy and therefore refuse to enforce any part of the contract including the arbitration clause. Or it could, as suggested by the question, regard the arbitration clause as severable from the rest of the contract, and remit the parties to an arbitrator in accord with their promise. This would not guarantee, however, that it would enforce any award that emanated from that arbitration. Certainly, if the arbitrator ruled in favor of Smith, the forum court could refuse enforcement of the award on the ground that the arbitrator was requiring Brown to comply with a contract which was illegal under forum law. An award favoring Brown would complicate matters, however. By enforcing the award, the court would be allowing Brown to escape the obligations of a contract that the forum regarded as illegal. However, the forum court might conclude that because such an award would be based upon defective performance of that illegal contract, rather than its illegality under forum law, enforcement of the award would be placing the court's stamp of approval upon the underlying contract.

FAHERTY v. FAHERTY (Page 466)

With regard to the arbitration of alimony disputes, suppose an arbitrator rules that because of changed circumstances, a husband's alimony obligation of $600 per month should be eliminated; and that, despite the court's suggestion (but not mandate), the arbitrator makes no detailed findings of fact because neither party asked him to do so. Suppose further that, because of her loss of alimony, the ex-wife becomes a public charge, supported by the state's taxpayers. Should the court not have reserved the same powers of de novo review here, as it did with respect to an arbitrator's modifications of child support? Isn't the public interest sufficiently implicated to justify such a rule? Or are the statutory grounds for refusing to enforce, or for vacating, an arbitrator's award sufficient to meet the situation described herein?

NOTES AND PROBLEMS FOR DISCUSSION (Page 474)

Note 1 (Page 474): Although the court states that "We do not reach the question of whether arbitration of child custody and visitation rights is enforceable," it also states: "As we gain experience in the arbitration of child support and custody disputes, it may become evident that a child's best interests are as well protected by an arbitrator as by a judge." Taken together, the two statements indicate that arbitration of child custody disputes is permissible in New Jersey--although whether, and under what circumstances, the awards in such cases will be enforced will have to await further developments.

As to whether child custody disputes should be subject to arbitration, much depends upon the quality (i.e., training, background and integrity) of the arbitrators to whom such tasks will be entrusted. Because the custody issue is more sensitive, and has a greater social impact, than the alimony and even child support issues, an reasonable argument for different arbitrability standards can be made.

The standard of review is another matter. Although the court refers to a *de novo* (in addition to statutory) review of an arbitration award modifying child support obligations, its description of how that review would work differs sharply from what is ordinarily contemplated by a *de novo* review. Generally, a *de novo* review means a completely new trial. (Cf. the *de novo* trial granted from small claims court judgments, discussed at page 150 of the Casebook.) Here, *de novo* review will not be granted unless the award "adversely affected the *substantial* best interests of the child." Even if that hurdle is overcome, the question remains whether the court will conduct an entirely new trial on the child-support issue. If it will, then its recognition of the propriety of arbitrating child support disputes would be hollow. To avoid that conclusion, the court might give some weight to an arbitrator's findings. Significantly, however, the court does not say whether any weight, and how much, would be accorded the conclusions reached by an arbitrator. The adequacy of the standard of judicial review in child custody arbitration cases would, therefore, depend upon how that standard is ultimately defined.

Note 2 (Page 474): Because a mediated custody arrangement would be the parties' own, and an arbitrated arrangement would be imposed upon them by a third party, there is good reason to be more deferential to the former than to the latter.

2. ADHESION CONTRACTS AND UNCONSCIONABILITY (Page 474)

GRAHAM v. SCISSOR-TAIL, INC. (Page 474)

This case, like the others in this section, examines some circumstances under which an arbitration agreement might not be enforced by the courts. When enforcement is denied, a court in effect decides that the parties had not entered into a valid and binding agreement to arbitrate. In Graham, the question arises in an appeal from an order compelling enforcement of an arbitration award. The court notes (footnote 1) that under California law, no appeal lies from an order compelling arbitration--but that the validity of such an order can be reviewed in the appeal from the judgment confirming the award.

The court states that the invalidation of a contract on grounds of unconscionability is a "principle of equity applicable to all contracts generally." What purposes are served, therefore, by a finding that this contract is adhesive? One is that, in determining whether the contract is in fact unconscionable, its adhesive character will subject it to closer scrutiny than it would otherwise receive. Another is that if the contract or provision "does not fall within the reasonable expectations of the weaker or 'adhering' party[, it] will not be enforced against him"--a principle that does not apply to ordinary contracts in which the parties actually bargain (or at least have the opportunity to engage in meaningful bargaining) over each of its provisions.

As for unconscionability, the court draws a subtle distinction between two types of situations. Designation of an arbitrator who has an interest in the dispute or a relationship with a party which would otherwise disqualify him or her from serving is permissible, if it is done knowingly and voluntarily. However, no matter how knowing and willing the parties may be, they may not designate a party as the arbitrator or someone "whose interests are so allied with those of the party that, for all practical purposes, he is subject to the same disabilities which prevent the party himself from serving." The Union was found, under the facts herein, to fit into the latter category.

The broader principle announced by Graham is stated as follows: "[I]f a party resisting arbitration can show that the rules under which arbitration is to proceed will operate to deprive him of what we in other contexts have termed the common law right of fair procedure, the agreement to arbitrate should not be enforced." To be fair, a procedure need not fit into a particular mold. "It may be satisfied by any one of a variety of procedures which afford a fair opportunity for [a disputant] to present his position."

NOTES AND PROBLEMS FOR DISCUSSION (Page 489)

Note 3 (Page 489): In Painters Dist. Council No. 33 v. Moen, the California Court of Appeal distinguished the situation confronting it from the one in Graham. In Moen, noted the court, "[t]he arbitrator is not the union, and the agreement provides for a joint union-contractor committee, with equal representation from both sides. Arbitration panels of such composition have consistently been upheld in the past. * * * There is no requirement that arbitrators appointed by the parties or pursuant to an agreement be neutral or impartial, as long as equal representation is given to each side of the dispute." 128 Cal.App.3d at 1040.

Note 5 (Page 490): In Hope, neither of the parties had requested the procedure employed in Graham. Moreover, observed the court, "arbitration of the tort issues would be somewhat complicated by the nonarbitrable nature of related issues based upon petitioners' claim for commissions due. We consider that justice would be better served in this case by allowing petitioners to proceed with their action in court." 122 Cal.App.3d at 155.

Note 6 (Page 490): In Madden, the court observed: "[P]laintiff * * * benefitted from the board's assertion of equal power on her behalf, enjoyed the opportunity to choose from among alternative medical plans, and waived no substantive rights." As a result, it denied the claim that the contract was adhesive. If all the Madden factors were present in the case posed in this Note, it should go the same way--at least in California, and notwithstanding the more recent deceision in Graham.

Note 7 (Page 491): In Wheeler v. St. Joseph Hospital, the court stated: "Absent notification and at least some explanation, the patient cannot be said to have exercised a 'real choice' in selecting arbitration over litigation. We conclude that in order to be binding, an arbitration clause incorporated in a hospital's 'CONDITIONS OF ADMISSION' form should be given a reasonable explanation of its meaning and effect, including an explanation of any options available to the patient. These procedural requirements will not impose an unreasonable burden on the hospital. The hospital's admission clerk need only direct the patient's attention to the arbitration provision, request him to read it, and give him a simple explanation of its purpose and effect, including the available options."

In Obstetrics and Gynecologists v. Pepper, absent any findings by the trial court, the Nevada Supreme Court surmised that under circumstances similar to those described in this Note, it was "bound to presume that the district court found that respondent did not give a knowing consent to the arbitration agreement prepared by appellant clinic." The court therefore held that this case was governed by the principle in the California case of Wheeler v. St. Joseph Hospital, supra, under which "courts will not enforce against an adhering party a provision limiting the duties or liabilities of the stronger party absent plain and clear notification of the terms and an understanding consent." The contract was deemed adhesive because the "weaker party had no choice as to its terms."

<u>3.</u> <u>WAIVER</u> (Page 491)

<u>UNITED NUCLEAR CORPORATION v. GENERAL ATOMIC COMPANY</u> (Page 491)

The general title of this section, it will be recalled, is: "Have the Parties Entered Into a Valid Arbitration Agreement, and Are They Now Bound by It?" Waiver presupposes that the parties' arbitration agreement was valid, and that if one of them had insisted upon arbitration, rather than litigation, at the outset of a court suit, that insistence would be honored by a court. Despite an agreement's underlying validity, however, the conduct of a party may constitute a waiver of its right to insist on arbitration, as occurred in this case. The case is included primarily because of its synthesis of other decisions dealing with waiver. The principles governing waiver that are extracted from those cases are clearly set forth in the case itself.

<u>NOTES AND PROBLEMS FOR DISCUSSION</u> (Page 509)

<u>Note 2</u> (Page 510): In <u>Drake Bakeries</u>, the Supreme Court stated:

"[T]his Court has prescribed no such inflexiblle rule

rigidly linking no-strike and arbitration clauses of every collective bargaining contract in every situation. The company has not attempted, or claimed the right, either to terminate the entire contract or to extinguish permanently its obligations under the arbitration provisions. Instead, it has sued for damages for an alleged strike and, as far as this record reveals, the contract continued in effect, as did the promises of the parties to arbitrate and the promise of the union not to strike. Moreover, in this case, under this contract, by agreeing to arbitrate all claims without excluding the case where the union struck over an arbitrable matter, the parties have negatived any intention to condition the duty to arbitrate upon the absence of strikes." 370 U.S. at 261-62, 82 S.Ct. at 1351, 8 L.Ed.2d at 479-80.

Note 3 (Page 510): In Schwartz v. Leibel, the court notes the general rules that: 1) a right to arbitration is waived by bringing a suit on the basic contract itself without seeking arbitration; and 2) once such a waiver has been made, it cannot be revoked. 249 C.A.2d at 762-63. It held, however, that the plaintiff in that case did not waive his right to arbitration by commencing an action for injunctive relief in the superior court, since this was a form of protective relief which an arbitrator was powerless to grant, and was not inconsistent with the remedy of arbitration.

In Tas-T-Nut Co., the court observes:

"The right to arbitrate is of course possessed by each party to the agreement and notwithstanding one party may impede the normal course of arbitration such conduct cannot dispense with the right of the other party to compel it. * * * The utmost effect of conduct such as is displayed * * * here would be to give to the respondent an election to either insist upon arbitration or, acceding to the implied desire of the appellant, acquiesce in the abandonment of arbitration and resort to court action. But this is an election which it must make for it cannot keep alive in itself the right to arbitrate and at the same time deny it to its adversary."

G. THE ARBITRATION AGREEMENT'S EFFECT ON THIRD PARTIES (Page 511)

KAUFMAN v. WILLIAM ISELIN & CO. (Page 511)

"Factor" is defined in Neild v. District of Columbia, 110 F.2d 246, 259 (1940) as "[a] commercial agent to whom the possession of personalty is entrusted by or for the owner, to be sold, for a compensation, in pursuance of the agent's usual trade or business, with title to goods remaining in the principal and the 'factor' being merely a bailee for the purposes of the agency."

NOTES AND PROBLEMS FOR DISCUSSION (Page 514)

Note 1 (Page 514): The court's complete phrase is: "any affirmative action under the contract to enforce its terms." (Emphasis supplied.) This suggests that legal action by the factor to collect the moneys owed or to enjoin the buyer from disposing of the property in certain ways would qualify as such "affirmative action." In those events, the buyer could require the factor to arbitrate a dispute over alleged defects in the goods.

Note 2 (Page 514): Doyle v. Giuliucci held that a contract between an infant's father and a medical group for health care, which provided for arbitration of claims arising under it was binding on the infant. the parent's power to bind the child to arbitrate, according to the California Supreme Court, is "implicit in the parent's right and duty to care for the child." 43 Cal. Rptr. at 699.

HOWARD JOHNSON COMPANY, INC. v. DETROIT LOCAL JOINT EXECUTIVE BOARD, HOTEL AND RESTAURANT EMPLOYEES AND BARTENDERS INTERNATIONAL UNION, AFL-CIO (Page 514)

Like Kaufman v. Iselin, Howard Johnson explores the circumstances under which a person or entity may be bound by the arbitration promise made by another. The tension in Howard Johnson is between a federal policy strongly favoring arbitration of disputes over the interpretation and application of collective bargaining agreements and an equally strong policy to free business purchasers of burdensome contracts made by their predecessors. For an arbitration obligation to be imposed on a successor, continuity of the predecessor's operation is essential. As indicated by Justice Douglas' dissenting opinion, determining whether such continuity exists requires an examination of, among other things, the location of the new enterprise, the products and services it provides, the manner of production, the type of supervision, etc. What the majority adds here is the indispensable requirement of continuity of the predecessor's work force, apparently approving lower court decisions that have held a successor employer to be bound by its predecessor's collectively bargained arbitration obligation, where all other indicia of continuity are present and if the successor hires a majority of the predecessor's employees. The Court stresses, however, that as long as the successor does not discriminate solely on the basis of union membership or to avoid having to recognize the union, it need not hire any of the predecessor's employees, but is free to hire an entirely new work force. If it hires fewer than a majority of the predecessor's employees, it will not be bound by the predecessor's duty to arbitrate. As will be discussed in Note 5, infra, the Court also intimates that it might be inclined to hold that, even if a successor hires a majority of the predecessor's employees, it will not be required to arbitrate if they do not make up a majority of its new work force.

NOTES AND PROBLEMS FOR DISCUSSION (Page 524)

Note 1 (Page 524): The answer would appear to be clearly yes. At first blush, this suggests that the Court could have rested *John Wiley & Sons* on that ground alone. Why, then, did it examine the "continuity of identity" issue in that case? The answer lies in the fact that the rule that emerged in *John Wiley* was a *federal* common law rule promulgated under the authority that *Lincoln Mills* had discerned in § 301. Unlike the question of a statute of limitations in a suit against an employer that is not joined with an unfair representation suit against a union, see U.A.W. v. Hoosier Cardinal, discussed in the Notes and Problems for Discussion following *Lincoln Mills*, the need for a uniform rule on this question is compelling. It is important not only for the disappearing corporation and the merged corporation, but also for the union and its members, in guiding their "primary private activity."

Note 2 (Page 524): Crest-Tex, the assignor in *Kaufman* was not relieved of its contract obligations when it assigned the contract as security (and for collection if necessary) to Iselin. It is apparent, however, that Crest-Tex was probably "judgment-proof" in view of Iselin's need to collect on the contract, which would arise only if Crest-Tex did not repay the advances made to it by Iselin. That probably explains why Kaufman sought to require Iselin, rather than Crest-Tex, to arbitrate. Even if Crest-Tex were not judgment proof, however, the rationale of Kaufman v. Iselin rests on the doctrine that "no promise of the assignee to assume the assignor's duties is to be inferred from the acceptance of an assignment of a bilateral contract, in the absence of circumstances surrounding the assignment itself which indicate a contrary intention."

Note 3 (Page 524): The major practical problem Kaufman would have faced if it had tried to insert such a clause in its contract with Crest-Tex is that the latter would probably not have agreed to it. Having had to borrow the money from Iselin in the first place and assign the Kaufman contract to it as security, Crest-Tex was in no position to agree to any such contractual provision. As for a damage action by the union against the Grissoms, it would be barred by the arbitration provisions of its contract with the Grissoms. (See next case, Vaca v. Sipes.) Indeed, the Court relies heavily on the Grissoms' continued presence and possession of substantial assets as distinguishing Howard Johnson from John Wiley. It also states, however, that the Grissoms have agreed to arbitrate, and "presumably this arbitration will explore the question whether the Grissoms breached the successorship provisions of their collective bargaining agreements, and what the remedy for this breach might be." (Emphasis supplied.) In many cases, however, the time limits for arbitration will have passed. The damage action would therefore be precluded by a failure to exhaust the contractual arbitration remedy.

Note 4 (Page 525): Under the National Labor Relations Act, the NLRB has held that an employer commits an unfair labor practice in mixed motive cases (a valid business purpose combined with an anti-union purpose prohibited by the Act), unless the employer can prove that it would have taken the same action even in the absence of the unlawful motive. The Supreme Court has upheld placing the burden on the employer of making this showing, once the presence of an anti-union motive, as part of the employer's reasons for its action, is established. See NLRB v. National Transportation Management Corp., 462 U.S. 393, 103 S.Ct. 2469, 76 L.Ed.2d 667 (1983). To be sure, the question whether a successor has an obligation to arbitrate arises in a Section 301 suit rather than an unfair labor practice proceeding. However, as noted in Howard Johnson, the federal common law to be fashioned under Section 301 must be based on the policies of the federal labor law. It would appear, therefore, that the word "solely" cannot be relied upon to explain this apparent anomaly in the Court's analysis.

Another possible explanation may reside in the fact that the Court refers to "solely * * * to avoid having to recognize the union." One can argue that abiding by an arbitration agreement differs from recognizing a union--since the latter phrase generally refers to recognizing a union with respect to all aspects of the bargaining process. Indeed, in Burns Detective Agency, discussed in Howard Johnson, the Court sharply distinguished a successor's duty to recognize a union for bargaining purposes (which it found because a majority of the successor's work force consisted of the predecessor's employees in an appropriate unit) from the successor's duty (which it did not find because of its policy of not discouraging changes in enterprise ownership) to be bound by the terms of a collective bargaining agreement negotiated by the predecessor and that union. See also following Note.

Note 5 (Page 525): In N.L.R.B. v. Band-Age, Inc., the First Circuit held, among other things, that in a "duty to bargain" context, the percentage of a successor's employees who had been union members working for the former employer should be considered and not the number of carry-over employees compared to the size of the predecessor's work force. In Boeing Co. v. Machinists, the Fifth Circuit held that, in the light of the relationship between the predecessor and successor, the successor's employment of about 35% of the predecessor's employees did not establish a sufficient identity of the work force to require the successor to arbitrate under the predecessor's contract.

Although the Court distinguishes the Howard Johnson factual situation from the one in John Wiley & Sons, it indicates that it might eventually retreat from its John Wiley position. This is evident from the Court's concession that there is an apparent conflict between the rationales of John Wiley and the intervening case, Burns Detective Agency. Although Burns involved an unfair labor practice proceeding under the NLRA, its emphasis on the rights of successor employers to restructure the businesses they acquire, and thus not to be bound by a predecessor's collective bargaining agreement, would seem to cover the predecessor's arbitration duty as well.

John Wiley can be preserved, however, if the Court focuses on the special place arbitration occupies in American labor law. As noted in Warrior & Gulf, labor arbitration is a substitute not only for litigation, but also for industrial warfare--strikes, lockouts, boycotts, picketing, and the like. Moreover, in the Steelworkers Trilogy, the Court created a presumption of arbitrability with respect to the "issues" that parties intend to arbitrate under a broad arbitration clause. That rule undoubtedly requires some parties to arbitrate issues that they never really intended to arbitrate. The combination of these two policies might guarantee the continued viability of the John Wiley doctrine.

VACA v. SIPES (Page 525)

The context in which this case is presented should be emphasized. The section in which it appears focuses on the effect of arbitration agreements on third parties. Thus, Kaufman v. Iselin and Howard Johnson explored possible circumstances in which parties that had not expressly agreed to arbitrate, or had even unequivocally disclaimed their intention to be bound by arbitration agreements of others, might still be found to have an incurred an arbitration duty. In Vaca, by contrast, the emphasis is on the effect upon employees of their union's agreement to submit employee grievances to the grievance-arbitration mechanism established by a collective bargaining agreement--a type of provision that exists in well over 90% of such agreements.

The Court tells us (in dictum, to be sure, but highly authoritative dictum), that an employee who claims to have been discharged in violation of a collective bargaining agreement can not sustain a suit against his or her employer to vindicate that claim if his or her union's failure to take the grievance to arbitration was not a breach of the union's duty of fair representation. Moreover, the burden upon the union to establish that its conduct did not violate its fair representation duty is not onerous. The violation is not established by proving, as in this case, that the employee was not disabled in fact. A union violates its duty only if its conduct is arbitrary, discriminatory, in bad faith, or if it ignores the employee's grievance entirely or processes it in a perfunctory manner. At the same time, the Court emphasizes that had the contract not contained an arbitration provision, the employee could have sued the employer for breach of the agreement under Section 301.

NOTES AND PROBLEMS FOR DISCUSSION (Page 543)

Note 1 (Page 543): Employees form and join unions because they believe that their individual bargaining power (recall the "power versus reason" discussion in the Negotiations chapter) is far inferior to that of their employers, and that only by combining in a union can they redress that balance. Under the principles of the National Labor Relations Act, however, a union that represents a majority of employees in an appropriate unit (either by a secret-ballot election conducted by the NLRB or some other lawful route) becomes their "exclusive" bargaining representative. See J.I. Case Co.v. National Labor Relations Board, 321 U.S. 332, 64 S.Ct. 576, 88 L.Ed. 762 (1944). This means that rival unions are excluded from representing the employees while the union enjoys those rights. More important, it means that the employees themselves, who, before unionization, could negotiate individually with their employers about wages, hours and working conditions may not do so. Id. To be sure, NLRA

Section 9(a) permits individual employees to present grievances to their employer and to adjust them, as long as a union representative is given an opportunity to be present and the adjustment does not conflict with the labor contract. Nevertheless, the decision to take a case to arbitration is, as the Court notes in Vaca, generally retained by the union.

That principle of "exclusivity of representation" is generally not found outside the field of labor relations. While theoretically it is possible that members of other groups might voluntarily confer such powers upon their leaders, this would be extremely rare, and not compelled by law, as it is in the labor field.

Note 2 (Page 544): In Dober v. Roadway Express, Inc., the court made the following observations: 1) "In Hoffman v. Lonza, Inc., this court 'limit[ed] suits for breach of the duty to fairly represent to instances of intentional misconduct by unions.'"; 2) "[T]he darkest picture [the plaintiff] can paint is that the union * * * was inept, lackluster, careless; and as Hoffman and the cases following it make clear, negligence, even when gross, does not violate the duty of fair representation." For opposing authority, see cases discussed in Judge Cudahy's concurring opinion in Dober.

H. THE ARBITRATION PROCEEDING (Page 545)

1. SELECTION OF THE ARBITRATOR (Page 545)

BOARD OF COUNTY COMMISSIONERS OF NEOSHO COUNTY ex rel., BOARD OF TRUSTEES, NEOSHO MEMORIAL HOSPITAL v. CENTRAL AIR CONDITIONING COMPANY, INC. (Page 545)

NOTES AND PROBLEMS FOR DISCUSSION (Page 549)

Note 1 (Page 549): The meaning of the word "neutral" in both Section 20 of the AAA's Construction Industry Arbitration Rules and in K.S.A. 5-405, as well as in the arbitration agreement itself, determines the answer to the question posed here. Section 20 states: "In the event of a vacancy in a panel of neutral arbitrators * * *." (Emphasis supplied.) K.S.A. 5-405 says that the "remaining arbitrator or arbitrators appointed to act as neutrals may continue with the hearing and determine the controversy." (Emphasis supplied.) As a general rule, therefore, when each side appoints an arbitrator to represent its position, and the two select a third, it is only the third who can accurately be described as a "neutral." In that event, neither the AAA Rule nor the Kansas statute would permit the continuation and determination of the controversy by the remaining two arbitrators under the circumstances described in the question. This means that the Kansas common law would govern the situation, and pursuant to it, the remaining arbitrators would have no authority to continue hearings and render an award. However, because an arbitrator named by only one of the parties will sometimes rule against the party who appointed him or her, there is a question of whether mere appointment by a party necessarily renders an arbitrator non-neutral. The answer would require close scrutiny of the arbitration agreement to see what it contemplates with regard to the neutrality _vel non_ of any arbitrator who is appointed by only one of the parties.

AMALGAMATED MEAT CUTTERS AND BUTCHER WORKMEN OF NORTH AMERICA, NO. 385 AFL-CIO v. PENOBSCOTT POULTRY COMPANY (Page 550)

The discussion here, contrasting the situation in this case with the one in _Pluss_, again emphasizes the importance of an arbitration agreement's precise language on how arbitrators are to be selected. It also provides additional information on alternative methods of arbitrator selection.

NOTES AND PROBLEMS FOR DISCUSSION (Page 554)

Note 1 (Page 554): In _St. Luke's Memorial Hospital, Inc._, the Seventh Circuit upheld the Board's refusal to defer to the arbitrator's award. Although other factors were present, the court relied heavily upon the determination by the Administrative Law Judge that "the proceedings may not have been fair and regular because [the grievants] and their attorneys did not participate in the selection of the arbitrator who was selected by the Hospital and the Union president. The latter was known to be at odds with both employees." 623 F.2d at 1173.

Note 2 (Page 555): In _Texas Eastern Transmission Corporation_, the facts were similar to those posed in this Note, with one exception: When A notified B that he had selected D as his arbitrator, there were still four days left before the hearing date that had been noticed by C. Stressing that A had never "refused" to appoint an arbitrator, and that the contract did not indicate that time was of the essence, the court set aside the award rendered by C alone. Although, in the hypothetical case, A's designation of an arbitrator occurs on the same day that C is to start the ex parte arbitration, it still occurs before that proceeding begins. There is strong reason, therefore, to apply this precedent to this situation. By contrast, in Kentucky River Mills, A's reply that he recognized no obligation under the arbitration contract and that he refused to appoint an arbitrator resulted in the court upholding the award rendered by C.

Note 3 (Page 555): Recognizing the harsh effects of the clause that would permit a single arbitrator appointed by one side only to decide the dispute, the Fifth Circuit, in Sam Kane Packing Co., interprets it restrictively. "Once each side has named a representative we think the harsh penalty in allowing single party arbitration has fallen out of the contract. * * * [W]e hold that this one clause of the contract will be construed strictly to apply only where no representative whatsoever is named to the board." 477 F.2d at 1136. As for what the union should have done, the court's answer is "that the union should have sought an order from the district court compelling the company to follow the contractually agreed to procedures."

Note 5 (Page 555): Advantages of having permanent arbitrators: 1) They are more likely to have, or develop, a familiarity with the common law of the particular shop or industry; 2) Their permanency tends toward promoting greater objectivity on their part, since they do not have to worry about pleasing or displeasing either side; (this is tempered somewhat by the fact that "permanent" often does not really mean permanent; such arbitrators may be designated for limited time periods, e.g., five years; and contracts often provide that they can be removed from the permanent panel by either party without explanation). Disadvantages: 1) Possible tendency to decide some cases in favor of a union or employer only because a series of recent cases has been decided in favor of the other party; 2) The exclusion of ad hoc arbitrators many of whom might bring a fresh point of view to resolving particular disputes.

Bethlehem Mines Corporation rejected the claim that an arbitrator had acquired permanent status on the basis of custom and practice.

2. PROVISIONAL REMEDIES IN AID OF ARBITRATION (Page 556)

a. ATTACHMENT (Page 556)

COOPER v. ATELIERS DE LA MOTOBECANE, S.A. (Page 556)

Although this case holds that attachment is not permitted in an arbitration subject to the Convention, both the majority and dissenting opinions examine some situations in which pre-award attachment may or may not be permitted in a strictly domestic arbitration. At first glance, by its reliance on the Convention's language, the majority seems to imply that preaward attachment would be permitted were this an entirely domestic arbitration. However, that implication is negated by the majority's stressing that attachment is available only in damage actions, and its questioning "whether attachment is even necessary in the arbitration context. Arbitration, as part of the contracting process, is subject to the same implicit assumptions of good faith and honesty that permeate the entire relationship." Does the fact that as many as 85% of arbitral awards are voluntarily complied with negate the need of the prevailing parties in the remaining 15% to have some assurance that they will collect on their awards? Or would they be sufficiently protected, as the majority suggests, by the inclusion of security clauses in their agreements to arbitrate?

b. INJUNCTIONS (Page 562)

BOYS MARKETS, INC. v. RETAIL CLERKS UNION (Page 562)

At first blush, the majority opinion seems eminently sound. The union, after all, agreed not to strike during the contract in return for the employer's promise to submit disputes arising under it to arbitration. Does it not make sense to bind the union to its promise (and also to preserve incentives for all employers to agree to arbitration) by allowing a strike that violates the contract's no-strike pledge to be enjoined? The problem, of course, lies in the anti-injunction provisions of the Norris-LaGuardia Act. That statute, as indicated in Justice Black's dissent, was enacted to curb the abusive issuance of federal court injunctions in labor disputes. Moreover, in Sinclair, which is overruled in Boys Markets, the majority emphasized that the legislative history of Section 301 revealed that Congress rejected efforts to make a breach of a collective bargaining agreement an unfair labor practice, deciding instead to leave the parties to "the ordinary processes of the law." In addition, other provisions of the Labor Management Relations Act of 1947, of which Section 301 was a part, expressly waived compliance with the anti-injunction provisions of the Norris-LaGuardia Act.

A major point in Boys Markets, which is made even more explicit in the next case, Jacksonville Bulk Terminals, Inc., is that a Boys Markets injunction will issue only to preserve, support and protect the institution of labor arbitration. ("When a strike is sought to be enjoined because it is over a grievance which both parties are contractually bound to arbitrate," (emphasis supplied), "the District Court may issue no injunctive order until it first holds that the contract does have that effect * * *")

The Boys Markets rule is also another example of a federal common law principle--one overriding the express terms of a federal statute--devised by the Court under the power it derives from Lincoln Mills'interpretation of Section 301.

NOTES AND PROBLEMS FOR DISCUSSION (Page 574)

Note 1 (Page 574): American Eutectic Weldings permitted the lower court to enter a temporary restraining order "preserving the status quo" pending arbitration. Note also that the question of whether the arbitrator is empowered to order specific performance or injunctive relief can also arise. As a general rule, "an arbitrator may not impose a restraint upon a party to the arbitration prior to a final award." 161 A.2d at 367. The award, however, may provide such relief. The current Section 43 of the AAA's Commercial Arbitration Rules, headed "Scope of the Award," provides in relevant part: "The Arbitrator may grant any remedy or relief which the Arbitrator deems just and equitable and within the scope of the agreement of the parties, including, but not limited to, specific performance of a contract."

The provisional remedy, serving some of the same ends as an injunction, which is authorized by the FAA and the other Acts, is the stay of judicial proceedings pending arbitration. See FAA § 3. In Warrior & Gulf, the Supreme Court emphasized that arbitration in the labor field is a substitute for industrial strife, whereas in the commercial field, it is a substitute for litigation. Just as the Boys Markets injunction serves that goal in a labor context, so does a stay of proceedings under Section 3, and comparable provisions in state arbitration statutes, serve the goal of avoiding litigation that would violate an enforceable arbitration promise.

JACKSONVILLE BULK TERMINALS, INC. v. INTERNATIONAL LONGSHOREMEN'S ASSOCIATION (Page 575)

There are two major questions in this case: 1) Is the union's conduct a "labor dispute" as contemplated by the Norris-LaGuardia Act, so as to bring it within that Act's general prohibition of federal court injunctions in "labor disputes?"; and 2) If it is, does the Boys Markets exception for injunctions in support of arbitration apply here? The

Court's answer to the first question is that this is definitely a "labor dispute" for Norris-LaGuardia purposes because it is a dispute over "terms and conditions of employment." At this stage it makes no difference that the "underlying dispute" is over the Soviet Union's invasion of Afghanistan; the fact remains that the employer's effort to procure a federal court injunction against the strike under § 301, in which he necessarily asks the court to determine that the collective bargaining agreement forbids the union to refuse to perform certain work, makes this a "labor dispute." The Court also holds, however, that, although this is a "case involving or growing out of [a] "labor dispute," the strike itself is not over an arbitrable grievance. The reason: The union's "underlying dispute" is over the Soviet Union's invasion of Afghanistan. It is obvious that an arbitrator can not resolve that dispute; he or she can not order (at least effectively) the Soviet Union to withdraw its troops from Afghanistan. Therefore, since the cause of arbitration will not be served by enjoining this strike, the Norris-LaGuardia prohibition applies in full force.

Some students will ask: "But wasn't the question whether the strike itself violated the contract's no-strike pledge subject to arbitration? Why couldn't the court have authorized an injunction to prevent the strike on that basis? Wouldn't that have been in aid of arbitration and consistent with the _Boys Markets_ policy?" The answer is that for the Court to have permitted an injunction against the strike would mean that the contractual validity or invalidity of the strike would have been decided by the court, whereas the contract entrusts this matter to the arbitrator. The _Steelworkers' Trilogy_ teaches that the courts, in determining whether the subject of a dispute is arbitrable, should not decide the merits of the dispute. Although an arbitrator would not be bound by the court's determination in the injunction proceeding of the strike's validity _vel non_, he or she would be greatly influenced by it.

NOTES AND PROBLEMS FOR DISCUSSION (Page 587)

Note 1 (Page 587): The dissent's reference to _Allied International_ evokes several observations. The first is that the holding in that case demonstrates that the employer in _Jacksonville Bulk Terminals_ was not without means of redress for the union's violation of its no-strike pledge. Under the circumstances, the union's conduct constituted an unlawful secondary boycott under Section 8(b)(4)(B) of the NLRA. Section 10(l) of the NLRA requires the National Labor Relations Board to expedite the investigation of certain charges, including those under 8(b)(4)(B), and, if it finds reasonable cause to believe that the charges are true, to seek "appropriate injunctive relief pending the final adjudication of the Board with respect to such matter." Moreover, under Section 10(h) of the Act, Norris-LaGuardia Act restrictions on the jurisdiction of federal courts are expressly removed when they grant such temporary relief or a restraining order, or make and enter a decree enforcing, modifying, and enforcing as so modified, or setting aside in whole or in part an order of the Board. In addition, Section 303(b) of the Labor Management Relations Act permits those injured by Section 8(b)(4) violations to sue for damages in federal district courts without regard to the amount in controversy (or in other courts with jurisdiction of the parties).

This apparently chaotic pattern of regulations concerning the jurisdiction of courts to entertain suits involving strikes in violation of no-strike pledges is comprehensible if one focuses on the different purposes of the respective laws and judicial decisions. Because federal court labor injunctions had been prone to procedural and substantive abuse in the early years of this century, Congress decided in the 1932 Norris-LaGuardia Act to prohibit federal court injunctions in most "labor disputes" and to curb them drastically in others. After _Lincoln Mills_, labor arbitration became an especially cherished feature of the American legal landscape. To support that institution, _Boys Markets_ held that a strike that clearly violated a no-strike clause and that was over an arbitrable grievance could be enjoined pending arbitration, despite the Norris LaGuardia Act. In _Buffalo Forge_ (a sympathy strike) and _Jacksonville Bulk Terminals_ (a political strike), the "underlying" dispute was not arbitrable; therefore, Norris-LaGuardia prevailed in full force, and anti-strike injunctions in those cases were not allowed. By contrast, in _Allied International_, where NLRB proceedings were involved, Congress had made a deliberate decision to limit, by legislation, the scope of the Norris-LaGuardia Act. The damage action allowed under Section 303(b) of the LMRA represents a similar expression of congressional policy. It should also be recalled that even before _Boys Markets_, an employer could sue a union for damages resulting from its violation of a contractual no-strike pledge.

Although the majority in _Jacksonville Bulk Terminals_ does not respond to Chief Justice Burger's assertion that "[t]here is no rational way to reconcile this holding with _Allied International_," they appear clearly reconcilable if the above distinctions are kept in mind.

UNITED PARCEL SERVICE (NEW YORK), INC. v. LOCAL 804, INTERNATIONAL BROTHERHOOD OF TEAMSTERS, CHAUFFEURS, WAREHOUSEMEN AND HELPERS OF AMERICA (Page 587)

Among other things, this case suggests another potentially effective remedy for an employer if a union strikes in violation of its contractual no-strike pledge: namely, an expedited arbitration procedure. Of course, whether the parties provide for such a procedure depends upon their perception of how it would serve their respective interests, and their bargaining power during negotiations. If they do provide for expedited arbitration, however, it can be an effective substitute for a strike injunction: The arbitration can be speedily heard and determined; and, even without regard to the Boys Markets rule, the arbitrator's ruling that the strike violates the contract can be enforced by injunction even in the federal courts.

One stumbling block arises from the failure of the expedited arbitration procedure in this case to limit the amount of time that can be spent in hearing the case. Theoretically, an arbitrator could spend a whole month hearing evidence presented by both sides on whether what appears to be a strike is a strike in fact, and even if it is, whether it violates the no-strike pledge. Contracts that limit the hearing time in expedited arbitration are the exception, rather than the rule. However, the likelihood of prolonged hearings is remote, because a principal reason for parties agreeing to expedited arbitration is to minimize arbitration costs. Because labor arbitrators normally charge a per diem fee for each hearing day, the longer the hearing lasts the more costly will it be for both union and employer. (The usual arrangement is for them to share arbitration costs--although occasionally a contract will require the "loser" to pay all.)

The case also illustrates that the exception carved out by Boys Markets was very limited; other strictures, such as those under §§ 8 and 9 of the Norris-LaGuardia Act continue to apply even when a Boys Market injunction issues. The court's application of § 9 to prospective injunctions seems more sensible than that of either the Fifth or Seventh Circuit. It is also difficult to quarrel with the court's conclusion that § 8's "clean hands" provision is not limited to governmental arbitration.

NOTES AND PROBLEMS FOR DISCUSSION (Page 598):

Note 3 (Page 598): Advantages of expedited arbitration

in the labor field: 1) As discussed above, it reduces the arbitration costs (which often can exceed those of litigation); 2) It resolves disputes speedily, thus preventing them from festering and destroying the working environment; 3) For similar reasons, it is less likely to be accompanied by a strike in violation of a collective bargaining agreement.

Disadvantages: 1) The evidentiary record is likely to be less complete than in the case of regular arbitration (although, if there are no limits on the duration of the hearing, the parties can in theory at least present their cases as fully as they would in ordinary arbitration); 2) The parties may be tempted to prepare less thoroughly than in regular arbitration.

Outside the labor area, certainly the cost factor is equally present. There may also be many situations in which, after resolving a dispute, there is some urgency in the parties' need to get on with their own relationship or with their relationship with third parties.

3. SUBPOENA AND DISCOVERY (Page 599)

WILKES-BARRE PUBLISHING CO. v. NEWSPAPER GUILD OF WILKES-BARRE, LOCAL 120 (Page 599)

To avoid deciding whether the FAA applies to arbitration agreements in collective bargaining contracts, the court, exercising its § 301 authority, creates some federal common law governing the scope of the subpoena and discovery powers of labor arbitrators. It rejects the notion that broad discovery comparable to what is available in judicial proceedings should be available in arbitration--although it notes some arguments that have been urged in favor of full disclosure of facts prior to an arbitration hearing. Taking its lead from Supreme Court cases imposing upon employers, as part of their duty to bargain under NLRA § 8(a)(5), a limited form of discovery in aid of arbitration, the court holds that an "arbitrator may subpoena those materials he feels he must consider in resolving the issues presented to him. * * * [I]f a party must have access to the subpoenaed information in order to present intelligent arguments, the arbitrator may provide those materials." Here, because the arbitrator made no finding that the information sought was relevant, the court remands to the arbitrator so that he can consider that question and rule on the Company's objections.

NOTES AND PROBLEMS FOR DISCUSSION (Page 605)

Note 1 (Page 605): Based on the reasoning of Wilkes-Barre Publishing Co., the arbitrator could not issue the subpoena duces tecum. Wilkes-Barre, it will be recalled, relied heavily on principles evolved in cases decided under NLRA Section 8(a)(5). Detroit Edison is such a case. A court could therefore permit an arbitrator to issue a subpoena duces tecum, under the same circumstances that the United States Supreme Court had held that Section 8(a)(5) did not require the employer to produce the requested information, only if the FAA or a state arbitration statute authorizing such a subpoena applied to the case. The FAA's applicability is extremely doubtful in view of its "advancing lifelessness" in the collective bargaining area (see the earlier excerpt from Wilkes-Barre). As for state law, state procedural rules do sometimes apply in Section 301 actions (cf. varying state statutes of limitations in UAW v. Hoosier Cardinal Corp., supra). At the same time, to allow state law to govern the subpoenaeing of documents, or the pursuit of discovery procedures, when federal law would not permit this, would create the kind of disuniformity in applying Section 301 that was discouraged in Lucas Flour.

Note 2 (Page 606): Because the attorney has not informed the arbitrator why the information sought by the subpoenas duces tecum is relevant to the issues in arbitration, the reasoning of Wilkes-Barre Publishing Co. suggests that she should not sign the subpoenas. The union attorney should have accompanied the request with affidavits setting forth the kinds of information it is believed the subpoened materials contain, and why they would be relevant to the arbitration proceedings. When the attorney for the company learns that the subpoenas have been issued and served, he or she may request the arbitrator, in writing, to withdraw the subpoenas on the ground that the information sought is irrelevant. If the arbitrator refuses to withdraw the subpoenas, the company attorney can still petition an appropriate court to quash the subpoenas for the same reasons. All parties should keep in mind that the standards of relevance with regard to subpoenas are extremely liberal.

Note 4 (Page 606): Mr. Reynolds writes: "Far too often, arbitration becomes lengthy and expensive because the discovery occurs during the hearing instead of before the hearing. Certainly, minimal production of essential documents and correspondence is reasonable as long as the scope is carefully circumscribed. It is particularly appropriate from the parties and also from affiliated third parties from whom evidence must be obtained during the hearing. By the same token, discovery depositions of key witnesses may be helpful.

"Certainly, discovery that leads to prehearing disclosure of the issues, important documents and names of witnesses would be helpful in most cases except those that are extremely simple. Conversely, it would be counterproductive to have the extensive and far-reaching discovery that is so often used in the judicial process." Reynolds, Discovery in Arbitration, 18 The Forum 144, 145 (1982).

In Note, Relaxing the Standard for Court-Ordered Discovery in Aid of Commercial Arbitration, the author states: "Most courts, * * * fearful that prehearing disclosure will hamper the arbitral process, have imposed a test of strict necessity. This test is satisfied when a party can demonstrate 'extraordinary circumstances,' such as a danger that the information sought will no longer be available by the time the arbitral hearing begins." 50 Fordham L. Rev. 1448-49 (1982).

<u>CHESAPEAKE AND POTOMAC TELEPHONE COMPANY v. NATIONAL LABOR RELATIONS BOARD</u> (Page 606)

<u>NOTES AND PROBLEMS FOR DISCUSSION</u> (Page 611)

<u>Note 1</u> (Page 611): Section 7 of the FAA states, in relevant part: "The arbitrators selected * * * or a majority of them, may summon in writing any person to attend before them or any of them as a witness and in a proper case to bring with him or them any book, record, document, or paper which may be deemed mterial as evidence in the case." In view of that language, the decision of the federal district court holding that Section 7 "does not permit the enforcement of an arbitration subpoena issued prior to an arbitration hearing" is at least debatable. One can only speculate as to the reasons for the union's failure to appeal this decision, but it is not unreasonable to assume that doubts about the FAA's basic applicability to collective bargaining agreements may have greatly influenced its decision to seek relief from the NLRB in a Section 8(a)(5) proceeding, rather than from an appellate court.

<u>Note 2</u> (Page 611): The Second Circuit condones the union's making an <u>ex parte</u> request to the arbitrator that he postpone the hearing. From the arbitrator's viewpoint, the better practice would have been to give the company an opportunity to file objections to such a postponement. Although the arbitrator's decision on the postponement request would undoubtedly have been the same in any event, the company could not claim that the arbitrator was making decisions that vitally affected it without hearing its side of the issue.

Note 3 (Page 612): The main problem with the discovery right that flows from NLRA Section 8(a)(5)--there is a similar one that employers enjoy against unions as a result of NLRA Section 8(b)(3)--is that it inevitably requires a very long time for a definitive determination that the failure of an employer, for example, to make discovery violates its 8(a)(5) duty. Although the arbitration may be stayed, as in Chesapeake and Potomac Telephone Company, pending the resolution of the 8(a)(5) charge by the Board (and the courts), one of the main advantages of arbitration is lost in the process, namely that of expeditious dispute resolution. On the other hand, if broad discovery were permitted, without regard to the requirements of Section 8(a)(5) or 8(b)(3), it too could substantially delay the resolution of the underlying dispute. On balance, however, the likelihood of inordinate delay is much greater when the processes of the NLRB are invoked than it would be under a statutory right to broad discovery in arbitration.

It should be re-emphasized that, outside the labor field, discovery rights are practically non-existent. Therefore, when evaluating the efficacy and social utility of non-labor arbitration ("commercial," uninsured motorist, family disputes, medical malpractice, inter-corporate disputes, consumer disputes, etc.) against these features of judicial dispute resolution, the differences in the availability of pre-hearing discovery should also be taken into account.

4. THE HEARING (Page 612)

a. IN GENERAL (Page 612)

MIKEL v. SCHARF (Page 612)

This case is instructive for several reasons. One is that it is the first in the Casebook in which the arbitration panel is a religious tribunal. The other is that it quotes excerpts from the New York Act setting forth basic procedural safeguards in the arbitration hearing. Given the hostility of this religious tribunal to the presence and participation of an attorney in the hearing, how much attention is it, or a similar panel, likely to pay to the evidence developed in a subsequent hearing in which an attorney is present?

b. ADJOURNMENT (Page 613)

TUBE & STEEL CORPORATION OF AMERICA v. CHICAGO CARBON STEEL PRODUCTS (Page 613)

This is an extreme case of a violation of FAA Section 10. Not only did the respondent have good cause for requesting the postponement, but it was prejudiced by the refusal to grant it, and the only apparent reason for that refusal was to suit the arbitrator's convenience. As the following Note case indicates, a change in any one of these factors can lead to a different result.

NOTES AND PROBLEMS FOR DISCUSSION (Page 616)

Note 1 (Page 616): Allendale Nursing held that, where the employer had not been the cause of most of the prior adjournments of the hearing, it was an abuse of discretion for the arbitrator to refuse to grant an adjournment under the circumstances described in this Note. The award favoring the union was therefore vacated.

c. NOTICE (Page 617)

CASUALTY INDEMNITY EXCHANGE v. YOTHER (Page 617)

Notwithstanding the court's recognition of basic differences between appraisal and arbitration, the court concludes that under the circumstances of this case, the insured was entitled to notice of a hearing and an opportunity to present evidence as to the value of the stolen tractor. Here, as in the Minnesota case, only one appraiser was familiar with the tractor's condition, but the contract required two appraisers to agree on its value. The court refers to the use of the term "arbitration" by both the insurance company and the insured in their correspondence? Would that be sufficient to transmute an appraisal, which is what the insurance contract called for, into an arbitration? The court does not say that it does, holding only that, regardless of whether this is an apppraisal or an arbitration, the insured had to be given notice and an opportunity to be heard.

P.J. O'NEIL v. PUBLIC LAW BOARD No. 550 (Page 622)

NOTES AND PROBLEMS FOR DISCUSSION (Page 626)

Note 1 (Page 626): A union's constitution and by-laws constitutes a contract between the union and its members. Especially in light of the Supreme Court's statements in Burley I, the Seventh Circuit's disposition of the question appears more justifiable than the Sixth Circuit's. Moreover, even if the constitution did not contain the indicated language, a court could reasonably hold that notice to the union was a sufficient substitute for notice to the employee, if that practice was, according to the Supreme Court in *Burley II*, sanctioned by "custom and usage."

With respect to contracts covered by the NLRA, it should be noted first that the court in the next case holds, on the basis of Section 9(a) of the Act, that the "right of an individual grievant to be present for the prosecution of his grievance [and presumably to be notified of its prosecution] is a basic, fundamental right secured by the national labor law." Even if that right could be overriden by a union's constitution, non-members would not be bound by those provisions. It is also doubtful that they could be deprived of notice of an arbitration hearing involving their personal grievances by "custom and usage." Although opinions differ on this, the ostensible purpose of § 14(b) is to promote employee "free choice." That goal is incompatabile with any rule that deprives employees who choose not to join a union of their rights to be notified of, and to participate in, the prosecution of their grievances.

Even with regard to union members, whether the principles of the two *Burley* cases, which were decided under the Railway Labor Act, apply also to cases under the National Labor Relations Act is debatable. Section 9(a) provides: "That any individual employee or a group of employees shall have the right *at any time* to present grievances and to have them adjusted, *without the intervention* of the bargaining representative, as long as the *adjustment* is not inconsistent with the terms of a collective-bargaining contract or agreement then in effect . . ." (Emphasis supplied.)

Although not free of doubt (see Seymour v. Olin, *infra*), the emphasized words strongly suggest that a union constitutional provision or by-law depriving a member of the right to be notified of, and be present, at the prosecution of his or her grievance would be invalid. Moreover, writing about suits for breach of a union's duty of fair representation, Professor Robert Gorman, citing cases, suggests that "the courts apppear willing--in policing union conduct that is 'arbitrary and perfunctory'--to look beyond the question whether the union in fact pursues an employee's grievance (contractual or statutory) and to determine whether the union has made a full investigation, *has given the grievant notice and an opportunity to participate*, has mustered colorable arguments and has refuted insubstantial arguments by the employer." Robert Gorman, Labor Law 718 (Emphasis supplied).

d. *PRESENCE* (Page 627)

LOCAL UNION 1110, UNITED MINE WORKERS OF AMERICA v. CONSOLIDATION COAL COMPANY (Page 627)

NOTES AND PROBLEMS FOR DISCUSSION (Page 629)

Note 1 (Page 629): Unless the proferred testimony of the grievants was properly excluded on grounds of irrelevancy or immateriality, the award should be vacated.

Note 2 (Page 629): If the union's decision not to permit grievants to testify was based on good-faith strategic or tacitcal considerations, the union should prevail. However, if it was based on hostility, bad faith, discrimination, or perfunctory treatment of the grievance, the union would be liable for breach of its duty of fair representation.

Note 3 (Page 630): A strong argument can be made to support an arbitrator's decision to abide by the union's choice in this matter. The union representatives might have decided that the grievants would make poor witnesses in their own behalf, and essentially ruin the union's case. There is no way for the arbitrator to second-guess the union on this without running the risk of being adversely prejudiced if the grievants turn out to be self-defeating witnesses.

Note 4 (Page 630): It would lend further support to an arbitrator's decision to abide by the union's preference that the grievants not testify in the arbitration proceeding.

DEMINGS v. CITY OF ECORSE (Page 630)

The problem in this case differs fundamentally from that in the last few cases. Here it is not the grievant who is complaining about being excluded from an arbitration hearing. Rather, it is an employee who could be adversely affected by an arbitrator's award favoring the grievant. This situation arises most often when the grievance is based on an alleged violation of a contract's seniority provisions in an employer's layoff or promotional decision. If the grievant prevails, the employer will have to lay off, or rescind the promotion of, another employee. The union, of course, owes a duty of fair representation to both employees. The fundamental question here is whether the employee who might be adversely affected by the award has a right to be present and present his or her arguments to the arbitrator.

NOTES AND PROBLEMS FOR DISCUSSION (Page 634)

Note 1 (Page 634): The only question facing the arbitrator is whether the contract was violated when the grievant was not promoted. The adversely affected third party's interests are not unrepresented in the arbitration hearing. If the employer is resisting the union's claim of a contract violation to the point of allowing it to go to arbitration, it is reasonable to presume that it will adequately represent the interests of that third party. Nothing would prevent the employer from calling the third party as <u>its</u> witness, if the testimony to be given by the latter will be material and relevant to the issue in the case.

<u>e.</u> <u>COUNSEL</u> (Page 635)

<u>1.</u> <u>PRESENCE</u> <u>OF</u> <u>COUNSEL</u> (Page 635)

<u>SEYMOUR</u> <u>v.</u> <u>OLIN</u> <u>CORPORATION</u> (Page 635)

The court holds that the union's refusal to process the employee's grievance unless he agreed not to consult an attorney with respect to his discharge was properly found by the jury to have violated the union's duty of fair representation. At the same time, the court acknowledges that, in view of the union's role as exclusive bargaining representative, it could "limit the participation of privately retained counsel in grievance proceedings." The most intriguing question is posed in footnote 5, namely, "whether the Union may prohibit the mere <u>presence</u> of private counsel at grievance proceedings or meetings, even when the attorney takes no active role." The court suggests that the answer depends upon "an analysis of the collective bargaining agreement and the particular facts presented by the individual case." In the light of the court's discussion, various potential situations can be explored: 1) where the grievant faces potential criminal charges; 2) where a stenographic record of the hearing is not being kept, and there is reason to believe that the union representative is hostile toward the grievant; 3) where the collective bargaining agreement does not expressly state that the union will decide which cases to appeal to arbitration.

The union as such is not an attorney. Nevertheless, by performing the spokesperson's role on behalf of the grievant in arbitration, it essentially serves a similar function (often, but not always, with the aid of real lawyers). This role of the union as "counsel" is pertinent to the issues in the next case, Hines v. Anchor Motor Freight, Inc., which examines the question of the right to effective assistance of "counsel."

NOTES AND PROBLEMS FOR DISCUSSION (Page 642)

Note 3 (Page 643): The cited discussion by Arbitrator Simons suggests: 1) efforts be made to arrange either that "union counsel presents the case with private counsel merely observing, or vice versa;" 2) that private counsel's appearance be noted on the record; 3) that the record clearly show "that the union has offered to represent grievant and that grievant has declined such representation;" and 4) that unions continue "to follow the course of either permitting private counsel to remain as an observer while they present the case or vice versa."

f. EFFECTIVE ASSISTANCE OF COUNSEL (Page 643)

HINES v. ANCHOR MOTOR FREIGHT, INC. (Page 643)

Despite a clause in the contract making arbitration awards final and binding, and notwithstanding the employer's non-complicity in the union's breach of its duty of fair representation in the arbitration proceeding, the Court holds that the union's breach permits the aggrieved employee to sue not only the union, but the employer as well. For present purposes, the more fundamental question raised by the case, which is discussed in Note 1, infra, is precisely what kind of union conduct in, and related to, the arbitration hearing violates the fair representation duty.

NOTES AND PROBLEMS FOR DISCUSSION (Page 653)

Note 1 (Page 653): Justice Rehnquist suggests, in dissent, that the Court's decision is based on what it perceives as "ineffective presentation of the case by" the grievant's attorney, namely the union. Elswhere, he states that the claim is that the "arbitration decision should be vacated because the employee did not receive 'fair representation' from the Union in the sense of representation by counsel at trial." The majority does not expressly reject these characterizations. Yet a close reading of the case indicates that "something more" may, indeed, be required before a union can be found to have violated its fair representation duty. The majority, for example, endorses the District Court's view that breach of the union's duty "involves more than demonstrating mere errors in judgment." It states: "The grievance processes cannot be expected to be error-free. The finality provision has sufficient force to surmount occasional instances of mistake. But it is quite another matter to suggest that erroneous arbitration decisions must stand even though the employee's representation by the Union has been dishonest, in bad faith, or discriminatory; for in that event error and injustice of the grossest sort would multiply." (Emphasis supplied.)

To be sure, the Court repeats the Vaca formula that "a union may not arbitrarily ignore a meritorious grievance or process it in a perfunctory fashion." At the same time, it stresses the factors set forth in the previous paragraph. In view of that emphasis, perhaps the most crucial allegation of those relied upon by the Court of Appeals (see footnote 4), was: "the assertion that there existed political antagonism between local union officials and plaintiffs because of a wildcat strike led by some of the plaintiffs and a dispute over the appointment of a steward, resulting in denunciation of plaintiffs as 'hillbillies' by Angelo, the union president." It is not at all clear that proof of the other matters alleged in the complaint (see footnote 4), without proof of this allegation, would have been sufficient to establish a breach of the fair representation duty.

Note 2 (Page 654): In a non-labor arbitration, if the representative is an attorney, he or she would be subject to a malpractice suit if the quality of representation fell below what is reasonably to be expected of other lawyers. Whether a non-attorney could be held liable for malpractice is problematical. If a non-lawyer represents a party before an arbitration tribunal which regularly permits non-lawyers to do this, some objective standards of care could presumably be developed. The mere negligence of either a lawyer or non-lawyer, however, would not permit the vacation of the arbitration award or a circumvention of the agreement making arbitration the parties' exclusive dispute resolution mechanism. Nevertheless, in some situations, an award may be set aside, as where the "malpractice" of an attorney or non-attorney consists of colluding with the opposing party.

In any event, because the "representative" would not, in a non-labor arbitration, be imposed upon a party by statute regardless of his or her choice, there would be no comparable duty of fair representation.

f. EVIDENCE (Page 654)

HALL v. EASTERN AIR LINES, INC. (Page 654)

Despite the frequently heard comment that there are no rules of evidence in arbitration, this case illustrates that the exclusion of relevant evidence that, if admitted, would constitute a complete defense to an employee's discharge, violates the employee's rights to due process.

NOTES AND PROBLEMS FOR DISCUSSION (Page 655)

Note 1 (Page 655): The result would probably be the same under the Railway Labor Act, the National Labor Relations Act, and in a commercial arbitration conducted under the FAA. Note, however, that the erroneous exclusion of evidence justifies vacation of an arbitration award only if the exclusion substantially harms the party who sought to introduce it.

Note 2 (Page 655): The problem in this Note is essentially similar to one of the main problems in the following case. Its discussion can be postponed until after Emporium-Capwell has been read.

EMPORIUM-CAPWELL AND DEPARTMENT STORE EMPLOYEES UNION, LOCAL 1100 (Page 656)

This is the first and only complete arbitration award in the Casebook. It seemed desirable to include this case to acquaint the reader with what a labor arbitration award looks like, and because of its detailed treatment of several evidence issues that can arise in this field.

NOTES AND PROBLEMS FOR DISCUSSION (Page 675)

Note 1 (Page 675): Just as proof burdens vary in different types of judicial proceedings, so can they vary in arbitrations, depending upon the nature of the issue or issues in the case. The effects of a discharge, especially on grounds of moral turpitude, can exceed the mere loss of a job. Persons discharged for such reasons will often experience extreme difficulty finding new employment. Even if the discharge is based on other less serious grounds, a person's age, sex, religion, or national origin can sometimes prevent him or her from finding a new job, despite federal and state prohibitions of employment discrimination based on these factors. Therefore, to equate a discharge from employment with "industrial capital punishment" is not mere hyperbole--especially in periods of economic recession.

Note 2 (Page 675): The basic rationale for not permitting the grievant to be called as an adverse witness in Emporium-Capwell is that the information sought to be invoked is neither "material" nor "pertinent" to the controversy. The issue before the arbitrator was: Did the employer have sufficient information at the time it decided to discharge the grievant to justify the discharge? Because the employer did not at that time have any information that the grievant would be testifying to at the hearing as an adverse witness, the denial of the employer's request to call the grievant seemed appropriate. The issue can be elaborated by use of a reductio ad absurdum. Suppose the supervisor had dreamed one night that the grievant had stolen money from the cash register. On the basis of that dream only, the grievant was discharged the next day. Following exhaustion of grievance procedures, arbitration was invoked. At the hearing, the grievant was allowed to be called as an adverse witness, and on the stand, confessed to having stolen the money. The fact remains that the only basis for the action that the employer took was the supervisor's dream. It did not have the grievant's confession at the time it discharged the grievant. There is not likely to be much support for the employer's action under those circumstances which, in their essential respects, do not differ from those in Emporium-Capwell.

In Hoteles Condado Beach, a hotel lifeguard had been discharged because of alleged offensive sexual conduct in the presence of a hotel guest. The arbitrator's award in favor of the lifeguard was set aside by the federal district court in Puerto Rico for a number of reasons, including the exclusion of a transcript of a criminal trial of the lifeguard (on grounds that the arbitrator could not observe the demeanor nor weigh the credibility of the persons who testified at the trial). Observed the court: "Plaintiff submitted its case relying on the transcript; otherwise plaintiff could have taken other steps to prove its case before the arbitrator. * * * . The transcript represents the statements of various persons, given at trial, under oath, and subject to cross examination. As such, pursuant to Rule 803 of the Federal Rules of Evidence, it is admissible into evidence, even though the declarants are available as witnesses." The question of the transcript's materiality and pertinency was not raised in the case, however.

In Harvey Aluminum, because "[n]o evidentiary rules were announced prior to the hearing by the Arbitrator nor are there any provisions as to rules or law re evidence or procedure to be applied set forth in the agreement between the parties providing for grievance-arbitration proceedings," the federal district court held that the arbitrator's exclusion, as cumulative and therefore not proper rebuttal, of testimony by one of the employer's eyewitnesses denied a fair hearing, regardless of whether the testimony was proper rebuttal.

In Barker v. Government Employees Insurance Company, the

federal district court refused to set aside a commercial arbitration award where the arbitrator "showed his partiality and admitted certain records into evidence." Quoting language of the Second Circuit in Petroleum Separating Co. v. Interamerican Refining Corp., 296 F.2d 124 (1961), the court noted: "If parties wish to rely on such technical objections they should not include arbitration clauses in their contracts."

Two other items should also be noted: One is Rule 31 of the American Arbitration Association's Commercial Arbitration Rules which states, in pertinent part, that "[t]he Arbitrator shall be the judge of the relevancy and materiality of the evidence offered and conformity to legal rules of evidence shall not be necessary."

The other is that in the Emporium-Capwell award, the arbitrator concluded that the employer had proved its case, even without the aid of the grievant as an adverse witness. Only because the penalty of discharge was deemed too harsh under the circumstances--the grievant, whose work record was clean, was not discharged for theft but only for a violation of company policy leading to a loss of $40--was there a finding that the discharge was not for just cause, and that it should be converted to a four-month disciplinary suspension.

KARPINNEN v. KARL KIEFER MACHINE CO. (Page 675)

The court merely assumes, but does not decide "that an arbitration award may be set aside in a case of material perjured evidence furnished the arbitrators by a prevailing party." Elsewhere it states: "even if perjury be 'fraud' within the meaning of the Arbitration Act, [oral hearings on questions of alleged perjured testimony before arbitrators] should only be granted with reluctance * * * ." (Emphasis supplied). Whether perjury should be considered "fraud" under the FAA can be explored in connection with Note 1 following Karpinnen.

NOTES AND PROBLEMS FOR DISCUSSION (Page 678)

Note 3 (Page 679): In General Motors Corporation v. Mendicki, the Tenth Circuit held that a statement concerning an employee which was made in a conference and bargaining session to adjust that employee's grievance and which was clearly germane to the issues involved was unqualifiedly privileged and did not give rise to an action for damages. Noted the court: "We think Congress intended that the respective representatives of employer and employee at such conferences and bargaining sessions should feel free to express their respective contentions as to the pertinent facts and the issues involved fully and frankly and to strongly support their positions with respect to the controversy, and--employing the words of Mr. Justice Fortas in his dissent in Linn--do so 'untrammelled by fear of retribution for strong utterances.' Otherwise the chance for desirable fruitfulness from such conferences and bargaining sessions would be greatly lessened. Moreover, such actions for damages would create irritations between employer and employee, which would tend to impair the chance for a peaceful settlement of labor controversies between employer and employee in the future." 367 F.2d at 71.

Would similar considerations apply to non-labor arbitrations conducted under the Federal Arbitration Act or state statutes modelled on the Uniform Arbitration Act?

Note 5 (Page 680): a) In Grovner v. Georgia-Pacific Corp., the Fifth Circuit stated: "No authority is given for the bare assertion that unavailability of a transcript because of unequal financial circumstances causes an arbitration proceeding to be substantially inadequate. Nor has appellant demonstrated that in this particular case his lack of access to the transcript denied him a fundamentally fair hearing; it is '"idle speculation to assume that the result would have been different"' had appellant been provided with a transcript."

b) Tooley v. Martin-Marietta held that the union discriminated on the basis of religion in violation of Title VII when, without showing that it would result in undue hardship to the union, it failed to accomodate to the plaintiffs' religious "observance or practice," as is mandated by Section 701(j) of Title VII. The court determined that 701(j)'s accomodation requirement violated neither the "establishment" nor the "free exercise" clause of the First Amendment.

Section 19 of the National Labor Relations Act was amended in 1980 to exempt all employees belonging to a "bona fide religion, body, or sect which historically has held conscientious objections to joining or financially supporting labor organizations" from compulsory union membership--although such employees could be required to contribute an amount equal to initiation fees and dues to a nonreligious charity. Previously, Section 19 had applied only to employees of health care institutions. As part of the 1980 amendments, Congress also required employees who exercised their rights under Section 19 to reimburse their union bargaining agent for the cost of representing them in a grievance or arbitration procedure.

5. THE ARBITRATOR (Page 680)

1) CONFLICT OF INTEREST (Page 680)

COMMONWEALTH COATINGS CORP. v. CONTINENTAL CASUALTY CO. (Page 680)

The significance of the various opinions in this case is explored in the next one, Merit Insurance Company. It is therefore advisable to assign both cases to be read for a single class session. However, if that cannot be done, it is sufficient to note that there is no single rationale for the decision that commands a majority of the Justices in Commonwealth Coatings. It should be noted also that the main problem here is whether Section 10 of the FAA should be interpreted as imposing upon arbitrators the same standards that are applied to judges?

NOTES AND PROBLEMS FOR DISCUSSION (Page 686)

Note 1 (Page 686): All members of the Court agree that the Arbitrator was not guilty of actual partiality. However, the plurality and concurring Justices are concerned with the "appearance" of impartiality. This is difficult to reconcile with the precise language of Section 10 which speaks only of "evident partiality," which seems to mean partiality which both exists in fact and is evident to others--as opposed to a possibility of partiality, which is all that the plurality and concurring Justices appear to require for vacating the award under that section. It is clear that the arbitrator did not resort to "undue means" in his conduct of the hearing and his rendering of the award. Is the plurality saying that the arbitrator's failure to disclose his prior relationship with the prime contractor constituted "undue means?" Or is it intimating that "the award was procured by * * * undue means" because the prime contractor failed to disclose the relationship with the arbitrator? Can such a claim hold up in the light of the lower courts' findings that the arbitrator "was innocent of any actual partiality, or bias, or improper motive?"

Note 2 (Page 686): Although the precise holding of Commonwealth Coatings is murky because of the three approaches taken in the case, the admission by petitioner's counsel was obviously not ignored by the Court in reaching its decision. Although tending to overstatement of the Court's position, as dissenting opinions are prone to do, the dissent characterizes the rule that emerges from this case as follows: "[I]f an arbitrator has any prior business relationship with one of the parties of which he fails to inform the other party, however innocently, the arbitration award is always subject to being set aside."

<u>MERIT INSURANCE COMPANY v. LEATHERBY INSURANCE COMPANY</u> (Page 687)

The case contains at least one rather opaque observation by the court. "[T]hat 'appearance of bias' is a proper standard for disqualification of arbitrators," it states, "is not inconsistent with anything in our present opinion; it just means that it is unnecessary to demonstrate--what is almost impossible to demonstrate--that the arbitrator had an actual bias. The standard is an objective one, but less exacting than the one governing judges." What exactly does the court mean by that?

For one thing, despite the court's rejection of the <u>Commonwealth Coatings</u>' plurality rationale, this statement indicates that it does not disagree with the latter's emphasis on the "appearance of bias." More important than that, what it seems to be saying is that it is insufficient that there is an appearance of a remote potential of bias. What is required is that there be an appearance of a relationship between the arbitrator and a party, or one associated with the party, which is "so intimate--personally, socially, professionally, or financially--as to cast serious doubt on [the arbitrator's] impartiality."

Would the result in <u>Merit Insurance</u> have been different if, instead of being a $10,000,000 case, only $5,000 were involved? Wouldn't the costs of investigating the background of the arbitrators on the AAA's panel then represent a substantial portion of the amount in controversy, thereby discouraging such investigation? Under such circumstances, should the parties not have a right to rely upon the information revealed by the AAA's disclosure requirements, even in an FAA Section 10 motion to vacate an award or a Rule 60(b)(6) motion to set aside the award?

<u>NOTES AND PROBLEMS FOR DISCUSSION</u> (Page 696)

<u>Note 1</u> (Page 696): The question posed here is somewhat rhetorical. Contrary to what might first appear to be his message, Judge Posner is not suggesting that, in return for

the guarantee of an expert panel, parties to an arbitration are willing to relinquish their right to an impartial panel. This is clear from, among other comments, his statement that the result in Commonwealth Coatings, despite what he regards as its faulty rationale, was justifiable, "because the facts of the case required disqualification even under a narrow reading of section 10(b): the 'neutral' arbitrator was a regular supplier of one of the parties to the arbitration, and had even rendered services on projects involved in the arbitration."

What Judge Posner is saying in his "expertise-impartiality" discussion is that a major advantage of arbitration over judicial dispute resolution is the parties' ability to select the person or persons who will decide their dispute. Persons so chosen will ordinarily be experts in the particular field in which the parties are quarreling. In the course of becoming experts, however, it is likely, if not inevitable, that they will have become acquainted with one or more of the parties or have associated with others who have business relationships with one or more of those parties. While this may be sufficient to disqualify a judge from hearing a case (although not necessarily--see Chitamacha which "held that a district judge did not have to disqualify himself from a case in which the defendant was a corporation that the judge had represented when he was in private practice, since the representation had terminated at least six years before"), the emphasis in arbitration upon the decision-maker's expertise requires disqualification only if the relationship between the arbitrator and a party, or one associated with the party, is "so intimate--personally, socially, professionally, or financially--as to cast serious doubt on [the arbitrator's] impartiality."

Note 2 (Page 697): The Chitamacha case discussed in Merit Insurance and in the previous Note suggests that, if these are the only facts revealed in the proceeding to vacate the award, the motion to do so should be denied. Chitamacha, for one thing, involved a question of judicial disqualification, whereas here the question is the vacation of an arbitral award. Also in Chitamacha, the judge had terminated his representation of the party six years before; here, it had been nine years since Jones had been involved in labor relations. Moreover, in Chitamacha, the judge had represented a corporation which was now a party in a case before him. By contrast, in Jones' case, the corporation he had represented was not a party in the arbitration.

Can one properly assume that, because of Jones' prior

experience as a labor negotiator and grievance processor on behalf of management, he would be inclined to disfavor any union that appeared before him? The platforms of the Democratic and Republican Parties express different biases in the area of labor-management relations. Would an arbitrator's failure to reveal long-standing membership in the Democratic Party, or Republican Party, justify vacating an award that he or she rendered against an employer or a union, respectively?

MORRIS v. METRIYAKOOL (Page 697)

This case is both similar to and different from the last two, Commonwealth Coatings and Merit Insurance. In the earlier cases, the focus was on defining, under Section 10 of the FAA or FRCP Rule 60(b)(6), arbitrators' conflicts of interests. Here, the court is confronted primarily by a constitutional question. Composed of several parts, it essentially asks: 1) whether "state action" is present in the process of selecting an arbitration panel pursuant to the Michigan malpractice arbitration act; and 2) whether the prescribed composition of the panel (i.e., the mandatory inclusion of a physician or hospital administrator as one of the three arbitrators) deprives medical malpractice claimants of a fair and impartial tribunal in violation of the due process guarantees of the federal constitution's Fourteenth Amendment and of the Michigan Constitution. Also, in the earlier cases, the court was faced with efforts to set aside arbitrators' awards based on the alleged conflicts of interest. Here, however, the malpractice claimants are seeking to be absolved of their agreement to arbitrate, claiming, among other things, that because of the state's role in prescribing the terms of that agreement and the nature of those terms, to enforce it would violate their rights to due process. Analytically, this case could have been included in the section on the formation of arbitration agreements. ("Have the Parties Entered Into a Valid Arbitration Agreement, and Are They Now Bound By It?"). Because it raises the issue of arbitrator's conflict of interest, however, and because that issue could have arisen even after the arbitration was held, it was deemed desirable to place it here.

NOTES AND PROBLEMS FOR DISCUSSION (Page 727)

Note 1 (Page ___): A court majority holds, among other things, that the Medical Malpractice Arbitration Act did not deprive patients of a fair and impartial decision maker in violation of their due process rights. It is significant, however, that Judge Ryan does not reach this question, but concurs solely on grounds that there has been no showing of "state action." Judge Ryan's opinion is one of the most instructive on the murky "state action" problem, and is useful for the light it sheds on it. It is difficult to know how he would have voted on the "fair and impartial decision maker" issue had he found state action.

Note 2 (Page 727): The "state action" problem, as conceded by the U.S. Supreme Court and noted in Judge Ryan's decision, does not lend itself to easy solution. The question in this case is close. A strong argument can be made, however, that under both the "state command or encouragement of private action" and the "performance of a traditionally exclusively governmental function" standards, an important factor that should have been weighed by the court, but which was ignored, is the direct benefit of easing court congestion that the state obtained when it enacted the legislation. Also, under the "state command or encouragement of private action" rubric, there is a question of the relevancy of Flagg Bros. Here, unlike what was suggested in that case, we do not have a case of the state staying its hand as it does in applying a statute of limitations. Rather, the state is prepared to act positively through enforcement of any arbitral award that emerges from the state-prescribed procedures.

Note 3 (Page 727): Judge T.G. Kavanaugh apppears to believe that physicians function always as healers of the sick, single-mindedly dedicated to bringing the best medical care to patients, regardless of who they are. By contrast, M.F. Cavanagh stresses that physicians wear two hats, depending upon the circumstances. When they are functioning as physicians, one may assume that they are motivated as Judge T.G. Kavanaugh suggests. When they serve as arbitrators in a medical malpractice case, those assumptions are not necessarily warranted. What saves the statute, however, is that the parties need not agree to arbitrate in the first place, and the patient can rescind an arbitration agreement up to sixty days after he or she has entered into it.

Note 4 (Page 727): It is safe to assume that the Michigan Legislature was not motivated by a desire to create arbitration panels that would reflect particular biases. It is equally certain that the legislature was: 1) aware of the fact that arbitration of medical malpractice claims involve complex questions of law and medicine that require expertise in their resolution; 2) that lawyers would bring legal expertise to the panel, thereby assisting the non-lawyer members in reaching a legally sound conclusion; and 3) that physicians (or hospital administrators) would bring medical expertise to the panel, thereby assisting the members who were not doctors to arrive at a medically correct decision. As for the bearing of these probable motives on the constitutional questions in Morris, they would probably not affect the "fair and impartial tribunal" issue at all; regardless of the legislature's motives, the types of panel members it prescribes either have an inherent conflict of interest or they do not. A similar conclusion is probable on the "state action" issue--especially if one accepts Judge Ryan's characterization of what the U.S. Supreme Court had done in Flagg Bros. Under that interpretation, all the state would be saying is, "If you want our aid, then the type of arbitration panel you choose must be one that we believe guarantees a maximum potential for rendering true justice."

Note 5 (Page 727): There should be no change in the result under the facts stated in the question. In Commonwealth Coatings as in Merit Insurance, the losing party had not been informed of a direct relationship between the arbitrator and the opposing party. Here, the statute requires that the panel be composed of these classes of arbitrators, and all parties are made aware of that requirement when they enter the arbitration agreement. If a member of the arbitration panel had an undisclosed significant personal relationship with one of the parties, the award could be vacated under Section 10 of the FAA. However, that is different from the situation posed in this Note.

In the light of Keating, if a patient and a physician entered into a medical malpractice arbitration agreement that was otherwise covered by the FAA, would its noncompliance with the Michigan Act's panel "requirements" not prevent its enforcement in either a state or federal court?

Note 6 (Page 727): There are several important differences between attorneys' malpractice and physicians' malpractice suits. When attorneys are alleged to have committed malpractice, their injured clients are usually represented by other attorneys in an effort to seek legal redress in damages or some other forms of relief. Although the number of attorneys representing plaintiffs in attorneys' malpractice actions is not astronomical, it is substantial. Thus, there is no guarantee that if an attorney is required to serve on such a panel, he or she would have an inherent bias against attorneys' malpractice claims or be so concerned about his or her own malpractice insurance rates that the claimant would face an unfair tribunal. It is true, of course, that, even in medical malpractice law suits, some doctors do testify against defendant physicians. But the problem of finding such medical witnesses is perhaps only slightly less difficult today than it was when Dean Prosser wrote about it many years ago. Generally speaking, the likelihood of finding unbiased attorneys to serve on an attorneys' malpractice arbitration panel is probably much higher than that of finding unbiased physicians to serve on a physicians' malpractice arbitration panel.

b. ARBITRAL IMMUNITY (Page 727)

COREY v. NEW YORK STOCK EXCHANGE (Page 727)

NOTES AND PROBLEMS FOR DISCUSSION (Page 735)

Note 1 (Page 735): In Lief v. Brodsky, the court stated: "As a quasi-judicial officer, an arbitrator should not be called upon to give reasons for his decision. Inquisition of arbitrators, for the purpose of determining the processes by which they arrived at an award, finds no sanction in law. Shirley Silk Co. v. American Silk Mills, 257 App.Div. 375, at page 377, 13 N.Y.S.2d 309, 312."

In Griffith Co. v. San Diego College for Women, the California Supreme Court stated: "[A]lthough an arbitrator cannot impeach the award by testifying to his fraud or misconduct, his testimony is admissible to show what matters were submitted for decision and were considered by the arbitrators."

Note 2 (Page 736): In Greyhound Lines, Inc., the Sixth Circuit held that the arbitrator was protected by arbitral immunity from liability for acts committed while serving in his official capacity to break a deadlock between trustees; that ERISA was not intended to break the common law immunity of arbitrators; and since bonding was required to assure employees' right to damages as against those who "handle" fund assets under ERISA and an arbitrator is immune from such liability, bonding requirements applying to fiduciaries were inapplicable as to him.

BAAR v. TIGERMAN (Page 737)

NOTES AND PROBLEMS FOR DISCUSSION (Page 743)

Note 1 (Page 743): If the losing party in Merit Insurance had sued the arbitrator for damages, it would have been required to have first sought to vacate the award. Because, in the reported decision of the action to vacate the award in Merit Insurance, the court found that the arbitrator was not actually biased, the losing party would not be able to prove damages in an action against either the arbitrator or the American Arbitration Association.

Note 2 (Page 743): The refusal to grant a hearing is not a decision on the merits. A possible explanation for the court's decision not to grant a hearing is that, aware of the delicacy of the problem in the case, a majority of the California Supreme Court believed that its having to deal with the issue could be temporarily avoided if the plaintiffs lost at trial. If plaintiffs prevail at trial, however, a majority of the California Supreme Court could still disagree with the earlier decision of the Court of Appeal.

Note 3 (Page 743): Code of Civil Procedure section 1283.6 states, in pertinent part: "The award shall be made within the time fixed therefor by the agreement * * * ." By engaging the AAA to administer the arbitration, the parties agreed to the applicability of the AAA rules; indeed, the court holds that both the arbitrator and the AAA may be sued for at least a breach of contract because those rules were allegedly violated. If the Rules are modified along the lines mentioned in the Note, the parties will have agreed to them in the same way. Therefore, there would probably be no liability of either the arbitrator or the AAA under such circumstances. Only if the disclaimer of liability could somehow be found to violate public policy would there be a different result. However, no fundamental issues of public policy would appear to be involved in this situation. The Rules with respect to the time limits for an award concern the relationship between arbitrators and the AAA. Arbitrators who violate such rules may be dealt with by the AAA by being removed from its arbitration panel. If many cases of this sort were to arise and the AAA took no action, its resulting loss of reputation could lead to a fall-off in its business. The incentive for self-policing is clearly present.

Although Section 40 of the AAA's Commercial Arbitration Rules did not, at the time of the Baar decision contain such an express disclaimer, a strong argument can be made that it was implicit in the structure of the Rules and the relationship between the AAA, the arbitrator, and the parties.

Notwithstanding the above, a strong case can be made for the proposition that a limitation of liability in the AAA's rules would not protect an arbitrator who has deliberately violated one or more of those rules for the express purpose of harming one or more parties to the arbitration.

From the viewpoint of the "injured party," having the

right to withold payment of the arbitrator's fees might be regarded as a "reasonable" remedy; it would hardly qualify as "sufficient, however.

4. The Baar rule is likely to have some inhibiting effect on arbitrators' willingness to engage in the profession. Often, the designated time period for rendering an award is inadequate because of the complexity of the issues and the length of the hearing. At other times, an arbitrator (either full-time or part-time) may not be able to juggle his or her other responsibilities so as to make it possible to render an award within the designated time-period. To be sure, both the statute in Baar and the AAA's rules allow for extensions of time, but such extensions depend upon the willingness of the parties to grant them.

6. JUDICIAL REVIEW OF ARBITRATION AWARDS (Page 743)

UNITED STEELWORKERS OF AMERICA v. ENTERPRISE WHEEL AND CAR CORP. (Page 744)

This is the third case in the "Steelworkers' Trilogy," the others being American M'fg and Warrior & Gulf. The essential message of Enterprise Wheel is that the courts must largely defer to labor arbitration awards. Even though a court would have decided the case differently, and even though the basis of the award is ambiguous, the award is legitimate "so long as it draws its essence from the collective bargaining agreement." Of special note is the Court's observation that an award that is clearly based "on the requirements of enacted legislation" is beyond the arbitrator's jurisdiction, and should be set aside. The parties, after all, retain the arbitrator to interpret what is required by their contract--not what is required by external law. This seemingly straightforward principle is not without its difficulties, however, as seen in Note 4 following this case.

NOTES AND PROBLEMS FOR DISCUSSION (Page 747)

Note 1 (Page 747): By holding that an ambiguous award, which might be read as being based on the requirements of enacted legislation only or might be read as being based on the essence of the collective bargaining agreement, will be read as falling in the latter category, the Court does appear to create a presumption of the award's validity that is comparable to the presumption of arbitrability in the other two Trilogy cases.

Note 2 (Page 748): As is evident from the discussion in

Ludwig Honold Mfg. Co. the courts seem to be in great disarray on what facts will satisfy the requirement that a labor arbitration award be based on the essence of the contract. However, the standard enunciated in Honold's last paragraph strikes this reader as most consistent with what the Supreme Court intended in Enterprise Wheel.

Note 3 (Page 751): Suppose the contract in Torrington had included the word "express" before the word "provisions." Would that have allayed all doubts about the ruling in that case? Could not the union then have argued that such language created a negative implication that the arbitrator was authorized to modify implied terms of the agreement? Perhaps the best way for the employer to have assured itself that the arbitrator would not modify the agreement is to insist on language, in addition to the provision quoted in Note 3, that the agreement expressed the entire bargain between the parties and that it contained no implied provisions.

The Court's reference in Boys Markets to "a no-strike provision in" the contract in Lucas Flour is a strong indication that the Court regarded an implied provision as being "in" the contract. This would supply a persuasive argument that Torrington was wrongly decided. The main weakness in the Torrington result is pointed out by the dissent in that case; that result ignores what the Supreme Court said in Warrior & Gulf was a major part of the labor arbitrator's function: to apply "the common law of the shop and the industry."

Note 6 (Page 760): In W.R. Grace and Co. v. Local Union 759, 103 S.Ct. at 2183-84, the Supreme Court, in an opinion by Justice Blackmun, stated: "If the contract as interpreted by [the arbitrator] violates some explicit public policy, we are obliged to refrain from enforcing it. * * * Such a public policy, however, must be well defined and dominant, and is to be ascertained 'by reference to the laws and legal precedents and not from general considerations of supposed public interests.' * * *

* * *

"It is beyond question that obedience to judicial orders is an important public policy. An injunction issued by a court acting within its jurisdiction must be obeyed until the injunction is vacated or withdrawn. * * * A contract provision the performance of which has been enjoined is unenforceable. * * * Here, however, enforcement of the collective bargaining agreement as interpreted by [the arbitrator] does not compromise this public policy."

<u>CONNECTICUT LIGHT & POWER COMPANY v. LOCAL 420, INTERNATIONAL BROTHERHOOD OF ELECTRICAL WORKERS, AFL-CIO</u> (Page 761)

<u>NOTES AND PROBLEMS FOR DISCUSSION</u> (Page 766)

<u>Note 1</u> (Page 766): One can argue that it does both. On the one hand, it disserves arbitration in that the first arbitrator's award is not given preclusive effect in a subsequent arbitration proceeding involving the same employer and the same issue. On the other hand, because each individual grievance is separately arbitrated, the institution of arbitration is also well served by this rule, since the second arbitrator is allowed to exercise his or her judgment freely, within the limits of <u>Enterprise Wheel</u>, in resolving the matter in dispute.

<u>Note 2</u> (Page 766): The conflict with <u>Enterprise Wheel</u>, as the court itself acknowledges, lies in the court's examination of the merits of the respective arbitration awards. It suggests that, if the Clark award had not contained a cease-and-desist order, thereby granting prospective relief, it might follow the lead of other courts and simply hold that, although they contradict one another, both awards are valid, since each draws its essence from the collective bargaining agreement. Because of the Clark award's prospective relief, however, the court explores the merits of each award pursuant to what might be called a "rule of necessity."

<u>Note 3</u> (Page 766): Had the union sought and received judicial confirmation of the Clark award before the Bornstein award was issued, the Clark award might have carried the day. It is possible, however, that the union would have had some difficulty in getting judicial confirmation of the Clark award in its entirety. It will be recalled that in the proceeding that resulted in the Clark award, the union had rejected the employer's proposal that the decision in that case "be dispositive of all the grievances since they raised identical issues." In the light of that history, a court might have refused to confirm the cease-and-desist portion of the Clark award for exceeding the scope of the submission. Moreover, in Derwin v. General Dynamics Corportion, reported at page 774 of the Casebook, the First Circuit stated: "Only where an arbitral award is both <u>clearly intended to have a prospective effect</u> and there is no colorable basis for denying the applicability of the existing award to a dispute at hand, will a court order compliance with the award rather than require the parties to proceed anew through the contract

grievance procedure." (Emphasis supplied).

<u>SOBEL v. HERTZ WARNER & CO.</u> (Page 767)

Earlier decisions in the Casebook have stated that arbitrators need not write opinions explaining their awards. See, e.g., Wilko v. Swan, <u>Enterprise Wheel</u>. The <u>Sobel</u> case tells us why. "[S]uch a rule would undermine the very purpose of arbitration, which is to provide a relatively quick, efficient and informal means of private dispute settlement. The sacrifice that arbitration entails in terms of legal precision is recognized * * *, and is implicitly accepted in the initial assumption that certain disputes are arbitrable. * * * Given that acceptance, the primary consideration for the courts must be that the system operate expeditiously as well as fairly."

At the same time, the court recognizes that an award may be set aside for "manifest disregard of the law." How do you find out whether an arbitrator is guilty of this unless the arbitrator explains the reasons for his or her award? The answer is that you can't. What the court does is to engage in the sheerest kind of speculation as to what <u>might</u> have been the reasons for the arbitrators ruling as they did. If the facts adduced at the hearing provide some lawful basis for their result, then it will stand. Against that standard, it would be a rare award that would be vacated if it were not accompanied by an opinion explaining its basis. Moreover, as the materials in Note 1 indicate, even where the award is accompanied by an opinion, it will not be set aside if there is merely a mistaken interpretation of the law. Only if the arbitrator has manifestly disregarded the law will it be vacated. (Of course, as indicated earlier, an arbitrator's award ordering a party to commit an act that would violate a law will not be allowed to stand.)

<u>NOTES AND PROBLEMS FOR DISCUSSION</u> (Page 773)

<u>Note 2</u> (Page 773): The court's speculations (or, more charitably, its inferences) about what might have been the basis for the arbitrators' award were based on what appeared in these items of the record. In their absence, such inferences would be harder to draw. At the same time, there would normally be some indication of what the basic dispute was all about. The tone of the court's opinion suggests that it could have, and would have, reached the same result even without the mentioned items in the record.

<u>Note 3</u> (Page 774): <u>Sobel</u> draws a distinction between

remanding a case to an arbitrator to clarify what issues were decided, and remanding to have the arbitrator explain the basis of his or her award. In this Note, the potential issue is one of clarification. The word "potential" should be stressed, because on close examination, it is clear that the arbitrator's silence on the mitigation-of-damages point means that no such duty was intended to be imposed upon the grievant.

DERWIN v. GENERAL DYNAMICS CORPORATION (Page 774)

Among other things, this case reminds us that, although the FAA may be consulted in formulating federal common law in a § 301 suit, it does not apply of its own force. Therefore, the court holds that "the district court erred in dismissing the union's action to confirm as time barred under the one-year limitations period of 9 U.S.C. § 9." Whether confirmation is otherwise unwarranted implicates other considerations. Two federal district courts, the appellate court notes, have upheld a procedure of "confirming an arbitration award in a vacuum," as is sought in this case (i.e., "unlike the usual complaint seeking confirmation of an arbitrator's award, it does not seek resolution of a concrete dispute between the parties.") Those courts have then treated the question of enforcement separately. Although the First Circuit acknowledges that "this is a possible procedure," it holds that the better common law rule to formulate under Section 301, because it is more economical and less likely to usurp an arbitrator's role, is "to allow a substantial, or even unlimited, time period for filing actions to confirm (and enforce) awards, and to require that these suits, like others in the federal courts, allege a concrete violation or other dispute entitling the plaintiff to some relief."

Assume that the Derwin doctrine ultimately becomes the federal common law rule on this subject. Currently, in many states, parties who prevail in arbitration routinely petition for state court confirmation of the award at the earliest opportunity--although the losing party has not indicated that it intends to dishonor the award. The losing party will rarely seek to remove the proceeding to the federal court, and often the matter is decided by default. If Derwin survives, will the state court, under the rule of Lucas Flour Co., have to apply the Derwin rule if the losing party raises objections similar to those raised in Derwin? If the state court orders confirmation based on the losing party's default, could that order be collaterally attacked by the losing party in a subsequent proceeding on the ground that the state court acted in excess of its subject matter jurisdiction?

NOTES AND PROBLEMS FOR DISCUSSION (Page 785)

Note 1 (Page 785): The answer to both questions posed here lies in the following argument of the employer, as stated by the court: "The company views the union's desire to obtain 'paper' confirmation of the Stutz award as the first step in a clever ploy to subvert the arbitral process. Ordinarily, disputes involving the meaning and application of prior arbitral labor awards are themselves proper subject [sic] for arbitration. If judicial confirmation is granted, General Dynamics believes the union will come to court later with a host of grievances involving off-the-job passes, presenting the incidents as acts of contempt in violation of the order of confirmation. The company fears that this procedure will cause the court to lose its bearings and begin adjudicating disputes which should be handled through the contract grievance process."

a. UNTIMELINESS OF THE AWARD (Page 785)

JONES v. ST. LOUIS-SAN FRANCISCO RAILWAY CO. (Page 785)

The court formulates general rules regarding the timeliness of an arbitration award: 1) An award is invalid if it is rendered after the date set by the parties and if the parties have stated in unequivocal language that they intend the arbitrators to lose their jurisdiction if they render a late award; 2) Absent such unequivocal language, the arbitrator's authority will terminate after a reasonable time beyond the period originally fixed for the award has passed; 3) A sixty-day period is reasonable, but a 14 month period is unreasonable.

On this last point, the court appears to establish 60 days as the one and only reasonable period (i.e., a period of 60 or less days is reasonable, and any period longer than 60 days is unreasonable). By stating that "the 14 month delay here was clearly unreasonable," (emphasis supplied), and evaluating the situation under the Second Circuit's more flexible standards, the court might be leaving open the question of whether a delay of, say, 120 days, would be unreasonable.

NOTES AND PROBLEMS FOR DISCUSSION (Page 788)

Note 1 (Page 788): The Second Circuit's approach impliedly recognizes the difficulties arbitrators can experience in meeting strict time limits for rendering awards. Its rule accomodates both the parties' and arbitrator/s' interests, whereas the appparently inflexible rule of Jones (see discussion above) may not allow such accomodation.

b. POST-AWARD MATERIAL BREACH (Page ___)

LIBERTY LAKE SEWER DISTRICT NO. 1 v. LIBERTY LAKE UTILITIES COMPANY, INC. (Page ___)

Justice Holmes told us that "law is a seamless web." By delving into the mysteries of "fixtures," i.e., determining whether the personal property of A has become part of B's real property by being affixed to B's land, the case teaches us that, when an award requires performance by both parties, one party's inability or refusal to perform can excuse the other party's non-performance.

NOTES AND PROBLEMS FOR DISCUSSION (Page ___)

Note 1 (Page ___): It is doubtful that a refusal by the District to participate in the arbitration would be permitted by the courts under the circumstances described. There was always the possibility that the McHenrys could acquire these other easements before the arbitration hearing, or early enough in its progress to satisfy its obligations under the contract. In addition, there is a great likelihood that the District enjoyed the power of eminent domain, so that it could condemn those easements that the McHenrys might not have had at the time of the arbitration. Against that background, even with knowledge of the McHenrys' non-possession of several easements, the District might have willingly submitted the matter to arbitration.

c. REVIEW OF ARBITRATOR'S REMEDIES (Page ___)

1) ATTORNEY'S FEES AND POSTING OF BONDS (Page ___)

SWIFT INDUSTRIES, INC. v. BOTANY INDUSTRIES, INC. (Page ___)

NOTES AND PROBLEMS FOR DISCUSSION (Page ___)

Note 1 (Page ___): In John Wiley & Sons, a union sought to arbitrate a dispute with a corporate employer into which the original contracting employer had merged. The union "framed its issues to claim rights not only 'now'--after the merger but during the term of the agreement--but also after the agreement had expired by its terms." 376 U.S. at 554. As to the latter rights, the Court stated: "[I]t is reasonable to read the claims as based solely on the Union's construction of the Interscience [original employer's] agreement in such a way that had there been no merger, Interscience would have been required to discharge certain obligations notwithstanding the expiration of the agreement. We see no reason why parties could not if they so choose agree to the accrual of rights during the term of an agreement and their realization after the agreement had expired." Id. at 555.

In Enterprise Wheel, you will recall, the Court upheld an arbitral award that had been rendered subsequent to the termination of a collective bargaining agreement and which required reinstatement of discharged employees and back pay extending beyond the termination of the agreement. Commenting upon Enterprise Wheel, Professor Robert Gorman states: "[I]t is clear that if the grievance arises and the arbitrator is designated prior to the expiration of the collective bargaining agreement, the arbitrator does not lose his authority to render an award should the contract expire before he renders his decision; the impact of contract expiration upon his authority and remedies is a matter for the arbitrator himself to decide." Gorman, Labor Law 564 (1976).

As for the argument that the arbitrator had attempted to impose terms of a future contract on the employer, is not the remedy ordered here merely "compensatory," and therefore comparable to a back-pay order, which would clearly be permissible?

2) PUNITIVE DAMAGES (Page ___)

GARRITY v. LYLE STUART, INC. (Page ___)

NOTES AND PROBLEMS FOR DISCUSSION (Page ___)

Note 1 (Page ___): One possible distinction is that the alleged monopoly of the state to punish for wrongdoing may not be a total monopoly in fact. For example, the legally sanctioned excuses for homicide, as in the case of self-defense, although not expressly promulgated for the purpose of allowing private persons to punish others for their wrongdoing, nevertheless have that effect. More significant, perhaps, is a type of statute which would probably no longer be constitutional because of recent developments in sex discrimination and the law.

One such statute--and there were many others---was in force in New Mexico in 1970. It read: "Upon a prosecution for murder or manslaughter, in addition to other defenses which may be offered, it may be shown as a complete defense that the homicide resulted from the person's use of deadly force upon another who was at the time of the homicide in the act of having sexual intercourse with the accused's wife. In order for this defense to be available to the accused, the accused and his wife must have been living together as husband wife at the time of the homicide." N.M. STat. Ann.§ 40A-2-4(7) (1953) (Repl. 1964).

Does not the state, when it declares that an aggrieved husband's homicide under such circumstances will be justified in the eyes of the law, in effect delegate the right of public execution to a private person?

Note 2 (Page ___): Labor arbitration, we know, is a substitute not only for litigation, but also for industrial warfare. If such warfare were not suppressed by the arbitration-no strike-no lockout arrangement, unions and employers could, without violating any law, inflict severe economic punishment on one another. It makes sense, therefore, to allow them to delegate to a mutually selected third party neutral who is not a judge or other government official the power to punish economically either of them whose conduct that neutral has found to be willful or wanton.

7. ARBITRAL AWARDS: ISSUE AND CLAIM PRECLUSION (Page ___)

a. THE AWARD AND THE COURTS: COLLATERAL ESTOPPEL, RES JUDICATA AND WAIVER (Page ___)

VAZQUEZ v. AETNA CASUALTY & SURETY COMPANY (Page ___)

Although the award in this case was judicially confirmed, the court indicates that it would have reached the same result even if it had not been confirmed or reduced to judgment--at least in the case of a No Fault arbitrator's award. The court also suggests that, although the doctrine of mutuality of estoppel has been judicially repealed in New York, a favorable arbitration award in a no-fault arbitration proceeding may not be given collateral estoppel effect in a subsequent personal injury negligence case because of "the complexities of parties and subtle differences in issues." Here, however, the defendant and the issue in both are identical, and, because the court finds that the defendant had a full and fair opportunity to litigate the issue in the arbitration proceeding, the issues determined by the award are given collateral estoppel effect.

The principal message that emerges from the case is that arbitration awards may or may not have an issue-preclusive effect, depending upon a weighing of all the circumstances.

McDONALD v. CITY OF WEST BRANCH, MICHIGAN (Page ___)

NOTES AND PROBLEMS FOR DISCUSSION (Page ___)

Note 1 (Page ___): The process of judicial confirmation would transform the arbitration award into a judgment of a state court. An argument could then be made that the "full faith and credit" requirements of 28 U.S.C. § 1738 obligate the federal courts to give res judicata or collateral estoppel effect to that judgment. By stressing that the award in this case was "unappealed," the Court strongly implies that it would reach a different result if it had in fact been appealed and upheld by a state court. If that had occurred, the state court would have reviewed the losing party's objections to the award and ruled on them. Although an order of confirmation can be made without the losing party actually presenting his or her objections to the award, that party often has an opportunity to do so by resisting the confirmation petition. (FAA § 9 and some state statutes require notice of an application to confirm an award to be served upon an adverse party, but no such requirement is contained in the Uniform Arbitration Act or in many state arbitration statutes.) Is it not reasonable to conclude, therefore, that the order confirming the award would be equally entitled to "full faith and credit" in the federal courts under Section 1738--at least where the adverse party had received notice of the petition to confirm the award?

One possible problem with the above conclusion is the Derwin case which held that an FAA confirmation order will not issue absent a live dispute between the parties. Arguably, the respondent's assertion that the claimant intends to file suit on a statutory cause of action could satisfy this requirement. In the light of the Supreme Court's strong pronoucements concerning the statutes' policies, however, this might be regarded as an effort to circumvent congressional intent to provide a judicial forum for their resolution.

Note 2 (Page ___): A) It is not certain that the grievant would actually bring suit; B) The grievant may be satisfied with the result in arbitration; C) The agreement to arbitrate is the quid pro quo for the union's no-strike pledge. If the employer rejected an arbitration clause, the union could attempt to "persuade" the employer of the merits of the employee's claim by resorting to a strike.

Note 3 (Page ___): Given the Court's refusal to accord res judicata or collateral estoppel effect to an unappealed arbitration award, and its unwillingness in this group of cases to regard resort to arbitration as an election of remedies or a waiver of designated statutory rights, the admission of the arbitrator's decision in evidence would violate rules against the admission of hearsay and opinion evidence.

A strong case can be made for the proposition that the principle of arbitral immunity should protect the arbitrator from being subpoenaed to testify about his or her competence. Some aribtrators might volunteer as witnesses (in return for fees and expenses) to support prevailing parties' efforts to have courts accept their findings of fact. In doing so, however, they would waive their immunity, and would be subject to cross-examination aimed at establishing their lack of competence. Absent voluntary appearance by arbitrators, parties might try to establish their competence (or incompetence) by third-party testimony concerning their conduct in other arbitrations, copies of published and unpublished awards, and testimony concerning their general reputation in the arbitration community.

b. THE AWARD AND NLRB DEFERRAL (Page ___)

NOTES AND PROBLEMS FOR DISCUSSION (Page ___)

Note 1 (Page ___): It should be noted first that in Alexander v. Gardner-Denver, the Court rejected a request that it adopt a "deferral rule" for Title VII cases as the NLRB had done in *Spielberg* for unfair labor practice cases under the NLRA. The Court, in *Alexander*, stressed as its reasons for rejecting such a rule that: 1) arbitrators interpret the law of the shop, not the law of the land; 2) the arbitral process does not provide many of the procedural safeguards and advantages of a judicial trial. These reasons would appear to be equally applicable to the NLRB deferral policy, and a strong case can be made for the proposition that the NLRB's policy violates the letter and spirit of *Alexander*. One possible distinction lies in the fact that the NLRA is, in a sense, part of the LMRA, or at least very closely related to it, and that Section 203(d) the LMRA states in relevant part: "Final adjustment by a method agreed upon by the parties is hereby declared to be the desirable method for settlement of grievance disputes arising over the application or intepretation of an existing collective bargaining agreement." Although this principle would appear to be equally applicable to grievance disputes that also involve alleged violations of Title VII, the fact remains that Title VII is an entirely separate statute from the LMRA and unrelated to it, whereas the unfair labor practices set forth in Sections 8(a) and 8(b) of the NLRA are closely related, if not part of, the LMRA, in which Section 203 is found.

Note 2 (Page ___): The questions at the beginning and end of this Note are somewhat "rhetorical." The answer to each is obviously yes.

Note 3 (Page ___): If the arbitrator were to rule exclusively on the basis of what he or she believes is mandated by the NLRA, Enterprise Wheel would require the courts to hold that the award was not "legitimate." However, where the award draws its essence from the collective bargaining agreement, and the arbitrator also rules on the unfair labor practice issue, no such problem arises--at least as long as the NLRB deferral policy remains in effect. This is even more true if the arbitrator only "adequately considers" the unfair labor practice issue.

Note 4 (Page __): The Board is generally not in the business of interpreting collective bargaining agreements. Although it has the authority to do so when necessary, see NLRB v. C & C Plywood Corp., 385 U.S. 421, 87 S.Ct. 559, 17 L.Ed.2d 486 (1967), this is a task that is generally entrusted to arbitrators when the collective bargaining agreement contains an arbitration clause.

c. THE AWARD AND STATE COMMON LAW "WRONGFUL TERMINATION" ACTIONS (Page ___)

GARIBALDI v. LUCKY FOOD STORES, INC. (Page ___)

The main point of this case, for present purposes, is that the arbitrator's determination that Garibaldi was discharged for cause does not preclude Garibaldi from suing the employer for discharging him in violation of state public policy. Although the issue is phrased in terms of whether to apply a limitations period for appealing from an arbitration award, the court's discussion emphasizes one of the factors underscored in Alexander v. Gardner-Denver, namely that an arbitrator vindicates contractual rights only. By contrast, the courts vindicate statutory rights or, says the Ninth Circuit, even those developed by the common law process, and it makes no difference that those rights are state, rather than federal, rights.

The court's discussion of the preemption issue, though difficult and complex, could not be omitted here because it is closely linked to the arbitration question. Essentially, the court notes that the discharge was arbitrated under a collective bargaining agreement. It intimates that were that all that was involved, the employee's claim would be "federal" under Section 301, thereby preempting a state-law claim for wrongful termination. However, here, the state law claim is based on a violation of an important state public policy that is not aimed at regulating the employment relationship and is of great concern to the state. Moreover, to enforce it would not interfere with the federal policy favoring arbitration of grievances that arise under collective bargaining agreements, since the arbitrator would be focusing on contractual issues and a court on legal issues. Therefore, concludes the court, "[s]ince we find that the state claim is not preempted, we do not find the prior arbitration a barrier."

NOTES AND PROBLEMS FOR DISCUSSION (Page ___)

Note 1 (Page __): In Garibaldi, the court intimates in footnotes 9 and 11, and accompanying text, that preemption might be found in the type of situation described in this Note. State-law rights would not differ from those contained in the collective bargaining agreement. Since the agreement provides for ultimate arbitral resolution of grievances, allowing state courts to entertain the suit would interfere with what is essentially a federal claim.

Note 2 (Page ___): In Peabody Gallion, employees brought an action against an employer under an Oklahoma statute which prohibited discharging employees who made workers workers compensation claims. The Tenth Circuit upheld the district court's denial of the employer's motion for summary judgment. The Appeals Court held: 1) the statute was not preempted by federal labor law because it had nothing to do with union organization or collective bargaining and had no tendency to conflict with the NLRA or any federal labor law; 2) the binding arbitration clause of the collective bargaining agreement did not bar a remedy under the statute; and 3) the employees were not limited to arbitration as their exclusived remedy under state or federal law since the statute provided a substantive right that devolved on the workers individually and could not be raised under the collective bargaining agreement.

Note 3 (Page ___): In Olguin, the Ninth Circuit stated: "Garibaldi does not help Olguin, however, because Olguin's assertion is that he was discharged for complaining about mine safety conditions and engaging in concerted labor activity. Mine safety is governed by the Federal Mine Safety and Health Act, 30 U.S.C.A.§§ 801-962 (West Supp. 1983), and concerted activity is protected by the federal labor laws.

Olguin's remedies were provided by his employment contract and those federal statutes. Indeed, Olguin complained to both the NLRB and the FMHSA. He cannot now seek protection in state law, because he acted in behalf of no state law or policy. Arizona has little interest in enforcing federal law, even if that federal law is incorporated, as Olguin suggests, in the state's general public policy. Olguin explicitly invoked federal law in this cause of action and it was therefore removable, if not under section 301, then under the general federal question statute, 28 U.S. § 1331 (1982)." 740 F.2d at 1475.

8. MANDATORY ARBITRATION (Page ___)

a. PUBLIC SECTOR INTEREST ARBITRATION (Page ___)

DEARBORN FIREFIGHTERS UNION, LOCAL NO. 412, I.A.F.F. v. CITY OF DEARBORN (Page ___)

It is worth noting that, though referred to as a compulsory arbitration statute, the one involved in this case does not impose an arbitration obligation upon the parties if both object to arbitration. Arbitration becomes compulsory only if one of the parties requests it. Then, regardless of the other party's wishes, it must participate in the arbitration. Also, unlike some other "compulsory arbitration" statutes, this one makes the arbitrators' award final and binding.

NOTES AND PROBLEMS FOR DISCUSSION (Page ___)

Note 1 (Page ___): The first question posed in this Note is examined in footnote 56 of Judge Levin's opinion. He strongly suggests, but does not decide, that voluntary interest arbitration by a public employer would not involve an unconstitutional delegation of legislative power if "the authority of the arbitrator/chairman, freely chosen by the parties, can be confined to choosing between two alternatives, clearly defined before the public employer agrees to abide the result." This would appear to allow voluntary interest arbitration in the public sector only if it were "final-offer" arbitration, which was the type of arbitration contemplated by the Michigan statute at the time of this decision (see footnote 55 of Judge Levin's opinion). Implicit in this assertion by Judge Levin is the idea that voluntary public sector interest arbitration would be unconstitutional if the arbitrator/s had the freedom to resolve the dispute by compromising the parties' positions on different issues. Whether this is really what he meant is debatable, however, in view of the rest of his footnote 56, in which he notes that "[b]y agreeing to arbitrate, the public employer accepts a measure of responsibility for the scope of the decision."

Elsewhere in his opinion, Judge Levin emphasizes the difference between "grievance" and "interest" disputes, suggesting that the problems of an unconstitutional delegation of legislative-political authority would not be present in the case of compulsory grievance arbitration in the public sector. The quoted paragraphs from Warrior & Gulf suggest, however, that in the labor field, the line between grievance and interests arbitration is thin indeed. By applying the public sector equivalent of the "common law of the shop or industry," an arbitrator can, in effect, fill in the terms of a contract even while deciding a grievance. At times, this can have financial consequences for the taxpayers who support the public entity that may equal or exceed those flowing from an arbitrator's resolution of a bargaining impasse.

Note 2 (Page ___): As indicated in the next Note, Michigan established such a panel after City of Dearborn was decided. It could be argued that the arbitrator was in fact a party, and that because arbitration was compulsory, the union was an "adhering party." In context, however, neither of these arguments would prevail. With rare exception, public-employee strikes are prohibited by law. As mentioned in the opposing opinions of Judges Levin and Williams, compulsory arbitration was provided by statute to compensate for this prohibition of public employee strikes. Because the constitutionality of prohibiting public employee strikes has been consistently upheld by the courts, see, e.g., United Federation of Postal Clerks v. Blount, 325 F. Supp. 879 (D.C. Dist. Columbia 1971), aff'd without opinion, 404 U.S. 802 (1971), an imperfect substitute for the strike would be equally constitutional. While there is a latent element of unfairness in the composition of the arbitration panel, the alternative for public employee unions is to have no right either to strike or to arbitrate. Moreover, governmental arbitrators, although not enjoying the same technical independence as judges, will be motivated by a sense of professional responsibility.

Note 5 (Page ___): The reasoning behind the "final offer" arbitration device is as follows: If the union and employer know that the arbitrator is limited to choosing only the last offer of settlement which the arbitrator believes more nearly complies with the applicable factors under the statute, they will be restrained in the kinds of settlement offers they make. Thus, if either side takes an extreme and unrealistic position in the hope that the arbitrator will "split the difference," but the the other side's offer more closely complies with the statutory factors, the arbitrator will be required to adopt the other side's offer. The hope is that, as the parties exercise restraint in what they are willing to give or accept, many settlements can be reached by the parties on their own.

"Final offer" arbitration need not be limited to the area of public sector bargaining. A well-known example of its use in another field is that of professional baseball. Currently, after a major league baseball player has played for a team for two years, salary disputes may be submitted to final and binding arbitration. The arbitrator, however, is limited to choosing the best final offer made by either the player or the club. (Following the short strike of baseball players in 1985, a new contract was negotiated which, starting in 1987, provides for arbitration only after a player has been with a team for three years.)

b. MEDICAL MALPRACTICE ARBITRATION (Page ___)

BEATTY v. AKRON CITY HOSPITAL (Page ___)

Unlike the "compulsory arbitration" statute in *City of Dearborn*, the one here is entirely compulsory in the sense that, even if both parties prefer not to arbitrate, the statute still requires any medical claim to be mandatorily submitted to the arbitration board. The statute differs from the one in *City of Dearborn* in still another respect: Whereas in the earlier case, the arbitrator's decision was final and binding, here, although the arbitrator's report may be admitted as evidence in a jury trial, it is not.

NOTES AND PROBLEMS FOR DISCUSSION (Page ___)

Note 1 (Page ___): There is much strength in Judge Brown's argument underscoring the non-expertness of the panel. The mere fact that the statute does not preclude selecting true experts does not guarantee that they will not be selected. On the other hand, the fact of the panel's non-expertness can certainly be brought to the attention of the jury, and, given the proper instructions, it can be persuaded that it is not required to defer to that panel's conclusions. Also, the right of both parties, including the one who eventually lost in arbitration, to designate one of the arbitrators, and the admissibility at trial of any written dissenting opinion would provide an additional safeguard against a jury being unduly swayed by an arbitration panel's conclusions.

Note 2 (Page ___): There are several answers to this question: 1) Contrary to what is suggested above, the losing party may perceive that he or she stands little chance of persuading a jury to reach a different decision than the one arrived at by the arbitration panel; 2) As previously noted, non-binding arbitration, like factfinding and the mini-trial, may persuade the losing party that the dispute has been objectively examined by neutral third parties, and that their evaluation is, therefore, correct.

c. COURT-ANNEXED ARBITRATION (Page ___)

REPORT AND RECOMMENDATION ON EFFECTIVENESS OF JUDICIAL ARBITRATION (Page ___)

LINE & SHAPARD, EVALUATION OF COURT-ANNEXED ARBITRATION IN THREE FEDERAL DISTRICT COURTS (Page ___)

The procedures described in these two excerpts present some interesting contrasts. In California, the operative amount is $15,000, and sometimes $25,000. In the federal courts, it is $100,000 in two of the districts, and $50,000 in the third. In addition, in California the court's determination of the amount in controversy, which may differ from the amount demanded by either of the parties, controls. By contrast, in the federal courts, the parties control this issue; it is the amount sought in the case which determines whether it will be subjected to compulsory arbitration. (This may reflect the influence of the federal principle for determining whether a jurisdictional amount in controversy has been met. In that connection, the U.S. Supreme Court has stated: "The rule governing dismissal for want of jurisdiction in cases brought in the federal courts is that, unless the law gives a different rule, the sum claimed by the plaintiff controls if the claim is apparently made in good faith. It must appear to a legal certainty that the claim is really for less than the jurisdictional amount to justify dismissal." St. Paul Mercury Indemnity Co. v. Red Cab Co., 303 U.S. 283, 288, 58 S.Ct. 586, 590, 82 L.Ed. 845 (1938).) In California the arbitration is heard and the award rendered much sooner than in the three federal courts. And at least in the Connecticut federal district court, no penalty attaches to a party who does not improve its position after a *de novo* trial.

With regard to the "technical questions" posed in the Federal Judicial Center Report on the three federal courts, here are some possible answers:

Both in the state and federal courts, an arbitrator should have jurisdiction to award an amount higher than the limitation on the amount in controversy that governs referral to arbitration. All that limitation does is: a) (in the state court) to give the court a basis for deciding whether to refer the case to arbitration; that decision is not based on a full-scale hearing of all the evidence or a determination of the amount of an ultimate award or judgment; b) (in the federal courts) even though a party has demanded less than the amount that would foreclose referral to arbitration, FRCP Rule 54(c) states: "Except as to a party against whom a judgment is entered by default, every final judgment shall grant the relief to which the party in whose favor it is rendered is entitled, even if the party has not demanded such relief in his pleadings." This principle would appear to be equally applicable to court-annexed arbitration. Moreover, as noted in Note 1 following Taylor v. County of San Bernardino, infra, Cal. Code Civ. Proc. § 1141.26 permits an arbitrator to render an award in excess of the amount in controversy governing referrals to arbitration.

Concerning the propriety of the arbitrator ordering injunctive relief, Cal. Code Civ. Proc. § 1141.13 states that Chap. 2.5, setting forth the procedures and requirements for judicial arbitration, does not apply to any civil action that includes a non-frivolous or substantial prayer for equitable relief. Although the rules governing court-annexed arbitration in the three federal district courts do not expressly address this question, the policies behind the California exclusion would appear equally applicable there.

As for an arbitration award that is entered as the judgment of the court, the provision of the local rule that it "shall have the same force and effect as a judgment of the court in a civil action" strongly indicates that the award would have collateral estoppel effect.

<u>TAYLOR v. COUNTY OF SAN BERNARDINO</u> (Page ___)

This case underscores the differences between consensual judicial arbitration, and compulsory judicial arbitration. The court holds that the arbitration here was not court-ordered in the sense of being compulsory; therefore, the tolling provisions of the statute did not apply. Indirectly, this discussion informs us of the need to make some provision for tolling a limitations period when the arbitration is truly compulsory. As indicated in the court's discussion, the California statute does so provide.

NOTES AND PROBLEMS FOR DISCUSSION (Page ___)

Note 1 (Page ___): Because the proceeding is not a private, extra-judicial arbitration, but is court-ordered, a strong case can be made that the arbitrator should be empowered to award punitive damages. Again, it is important to keep in mind that a party who is not satisfied with the result in arbitration is entitled, as a matter of right, to a trial *de novo*. It should also be noted that, at least in medical malpractice cases, the California Court of Appeal has held that an arbitrator may award punitive damages. See Baker v. Sadick, 208 Cal. Rptr. 676 (Cal. App. 4 Dist. 1984).

If it is not frivolous or insubstantial, the judge should include the sum sought as punitive damages in his or her assessment of the amount in controversy.

BRIDGES v. CITY OF TROY (Page ___)

The case illustrates the risks faced by a party who seeks a trial *de novo* from an award rendered in a court-annexed arbitration where that party has lost on some, but not all, of the claims in the case. Under the New York practice, as interpreted by the court, although the defendant sought a trial *de novo* only on the claims it had lost in arbitration, its demand opened up all the arbitrated claims, even those that had been lost in arbitration by the plaintiff, and even though the plaintiff had not filed a demand for a trial *de novo* on those claims.

NOTES AND PROBLEMS FOR DISCUSSION (Page ___)

Note 1 (Page ___): First, there is considerable warrant for the assumption that California would follow the New York practice, based on the language of Cal. Code Civ. Proc. § 1141.20 (see Appendix M of Casebook), which states, in relevant part: "An arbitration award shall be final if a request for a de novo trial is not filed within 20 days after the date the arbitrator files the award with the court. Any party may elect to have a de novo trial, by court or jury, both as to law and facts. Such trial shall be calendared, insofar as possible, *so that the trial shall be given the same place on the active list as it had prior to arbitration*, or shall receive civil priority on the next setting calendar." (Emphasis supplied.)

Whether the defendant would be responsible for the arbitrator's fees and statutory costs under the circumstances described in this Note is problematical. Cal. Code Civ. Proc. §

1141.21 states in relevant part: "If the judgment upon the trial de novo is not more favorable in either the amount of damages _awarded or the type of relief granted for the party electing the trial de novo_ than the arbitration award, the court shall order that party to pay the following nonrefundable costs and fees * * * ." (Emphasis supplied).

Although the non-electing party improved his or her position on other claims in the _de novo_ trial, it is arguable that the above-emphasized language in Section 1141.21(a) would limit the inquiry in the hypothetical case to the relief that was granted to the defendant in arbitration, and whether with respect to that relief, the defendant improved its position. Whether the plaintiff had also improved its position with respect to other claims or issues would be irrelevant for these purposes.

d. GRIEVANCE ARBITRATION UNDER THE RAILWAY LABOR ACT (Page ___)

BROTHERHOOD OF RAILROAD TRAINMEN v. CHICAGO RIVER AND INDIANA RAILROAD COMPANY (Page ___)

NOTES AND PROBLEMS FOR DISCUSSION (Page ___)

Note 1 (Page ___): This is a rare example of compulsory "rights" arbitration in the labor relations area. As explained by the Court, the aims of the original Railway Labor Act of 1926 to prevent strikes in the crucial railroad industry were frustrated by the ineffectiveness of the voluntary boards of adjustment that had been authorized to resolve "minor" disputes (i.e., grievances). Only by making the process compulsory could these strikes be prevented.

Note 2 (Page ___): The 1934 amendments to the Railway Labor Act mandating arbitration of "minor" disputes at the request of one or both parties preceded the enactment of the National Labor Relations Act by one year. It also occurred long before _Lincoln Mills_, the _Steelworkerws Trilogy_ and other cases had exalted grievance arbitration for unions and employers covered by the National Labor Relations Act, and before the use of grievance arbitration had become as widespread as it is now. Although there is a strong likelihood that the vast majority of collective bargaining agreements between railroads and unions representing their employees would contain grievance arbitration clauses, even if the compulsory arbitration provisions of the Railway Labor Act were repealed, those provisions still prevent strikes over grievances in cases where such clauses could not be accepted by the parties.

Note 3 (Page ___): The Seventh Circuit, in Walsh v. United States, first noted: "'May' ordinarily connotes discretion, but neither in lay nor legal understanding is the result inexorable. Rather the conclusion to be reached 'depends on the context of the statute, and on whether it is fairly to be presumed that it was the intention of the legislature to confer a discretionary power or to impose an imperative duty.'" 723 F.2d at 573.

Interpreting the language and background of the New York Dock conditions, it concluded: "From this language, it is evident that the ICC intended the phrase 'may be referred by either party to an arbitration committee' to connote mandatory arbitration." Id. at 574.

Note 4 (Page ___): There is another basis for questioning whether the compulsory arbitration features of the Railway Labor Act are compulsory in every sense of the word. In the principal case, discussing the legislative history of the 1934 amendments, the Court notes that leading representatives of labor and management testified in favor of the provisions that would subject minor disputes to compulsory arbitration. Although railroad unions were not unanimous in their approval of the legislation, the vast majority agreed that it was a desirable amendment.

Note 5 (Page ___): When it comes to grievances, neither unions nor employers have any difficulty with requiring arbitration, as evidenced by its widespread voluntary use in industries covered by the NLRA, and its success under the Railway Labor Act. Compulsory interests arbitration is a different matter, however. Both employers and unions tend to believe that it is better to negotiate their own agreements, in the shadow of the threatened use of economic force by each side (strikes or lockouts) than to have the terms of their bargain imposed upon them by an outside third party. In recent years, however, a few unions and employers have abandoned this position. See, e.g., agreement between the United Steelworkers and U.S. Steel of a few years ago.

Note 6 (Page ___): In Republic Industries, the Fourth Circuit stated: "First, we think it too late in the day to argue that compulsory arbitration, per se, denies due process of law. * * * . [T]he Supreme Court, without discussion of the constitutional implications, has frequently enforced the provisions of the Railway Labor Act requiring binding arbitration of certain railroad labor disputes. * * * . Congress may require arbitration so long as fair procedures are provided and ultimate judicial review is available." 718 F.2d at 640.

The court then proceeded to hold there was no showing of bias in either the group making the initial determination nor in the arbitrator. "It is true that the 1980 Act makes the trustees' decisions presumptively correct * * * and provides that the decision of the arbitrator is also presumptively correct and may be rebutted only by a clear preponderance of the evidence. * * * Read together, however, these provisions do little more than allocate the burden of proof to the challenger and direct that issues which are close be resolved in favor of the nonjudicial dispute resolver. In this we perceive no evident unfairness." Id. at 641.

Note 7 (Page ___): It is doubtful that Americans with claims against Iran could have sued the United States in the Court of Claims for a "taking" during the period the Claims Tribunal was temporarily not functioning because of the incident described in the Note. Although their claims had not yet been adjudicated by the Claims Tribunal, it could not be said that they would not be adjudicated once the Tribunal started functioning again. The prior resort to the Netherlands' courts to set aside an award of the Claims Tribunal on Dutch internal law grounds could certainly be regarded as estopping the Iranian judges from asserting that Dutch internal law was not applicable to their situation.

As for a domestic tri-partite hearing in the United States, such an occurrence would undoubtedly permit an award to be vacated on due process grounds. The assaulting arbitrators would, of course, face possible criminal and civil liability for their conduct.

CHAPTER TWELVE
"RENT-A-JUDGE"

MONROE v. MONROE (Page ___)

NOTES AND PROBLEMS FOR DISCUSSION (Page ___)

Note 1 (Page ___): The appellate court's language is not contradictory. It emphasizes that, although the referee is a "court," i.e., a tribunal that decides cases like other courts do, it is not a superior court or the court of common pleas, but is specially authorized by the state constitution and statutes.

Note 2 (Page ___): Because the regularly constituted courts are bypassed by the reference system, the latter can properly be characterized as an alternative dispute resolution mechanism. The reference system lightens the case load of the regular courts.

Note 3 (Page ___): There are several major differences between an arbitration and a reference under a "rent-a-judge" procedure. In arbitration, the scope of judicial review is extremely limited. Under California law, by contrast, the referee/s' findings of fact and conclusions of law must be reported in writing to the court within twenty days after testimony is closed. Cal. Code Civ. Proc. § 644 states: "The findings of the referee * * * upon the whole issue must stand as the finding of the court, and upon filing of the finding with the clerk of the court, or with the judge where there is no clerk, <u>judgment may be entered thereon in the same manner as if the action had been tried by the court.</u>" (Emphasis supplied.) That judgment is subject to the same judicial review as any other rendered by the court, and can, therefore, be reversed on insubstantiality-of-the-evidence grounds. By contrast, such grounds may not be relied upon to vacate an arbitration award.

That the referee's findings upon the whole issue can be converted into a court judgment and is subject to the same standards of judicial review as other judgments sharply distinguishes the "rent-a-judge" system from ordinary arbitration. Ordinarily, because of clogged court calendars, several years will pass between the filing of a law suit, the holding of a trial and the rendition of a judgment. Under a "rent-a-judge" system, however, disputing parties can avoid this delay. By choosing a referee or referees, they, in effect, jump ahead of others who are waiting for their law suits to be set for trial. The result of the reference, when converted into a judgment, can be treated by either party as an ordinary judgment, but it will have been rendered two, three or four years earlier than if they had had to wait their turn.

The author of the Harvard Law Review Note suggests that California's "rent-a-judge" system raises additional constitutional law problems. "Trials conducted by privately paid judges raise issues of equal protection and due process. Closed hearings, such as those conducted in California, may also be at odds with the public's first amendment right of 'freedom of communication on matters relating to the functioning of government,'" quoting Richmond Newspapers, Inc. v. Virginia, 100 S.Ct. 2814, 2827 (1980) (plurality opinion) for the last statement. Note, The California Rent-a-Judge Experiment: Constitutional and Policy Considerations of Pay-As-You-Go Courts, 94 Harv. L. Rev. at 1601.

As for the policy considerations, the author states: "Referee trials * * * graft the private aspects of arbitration onto the public aspects of judicial proceedings. A referee's decision has all the authority of a judicial determination but is made within the private context normally associated with arbitration. Lacking the judge's ultimate responsibility to the public, the referee is interested only in solving the problem before him in order to maximize the satisfaction of the litigants who hired him." 94 Harv. L. Rev. at 1612.

Notes

Notes

Notes

Notes

Notes

Notes

Notes

Notes

Notes

Notes